IMAGES
of America

OLD CUCAMONGA

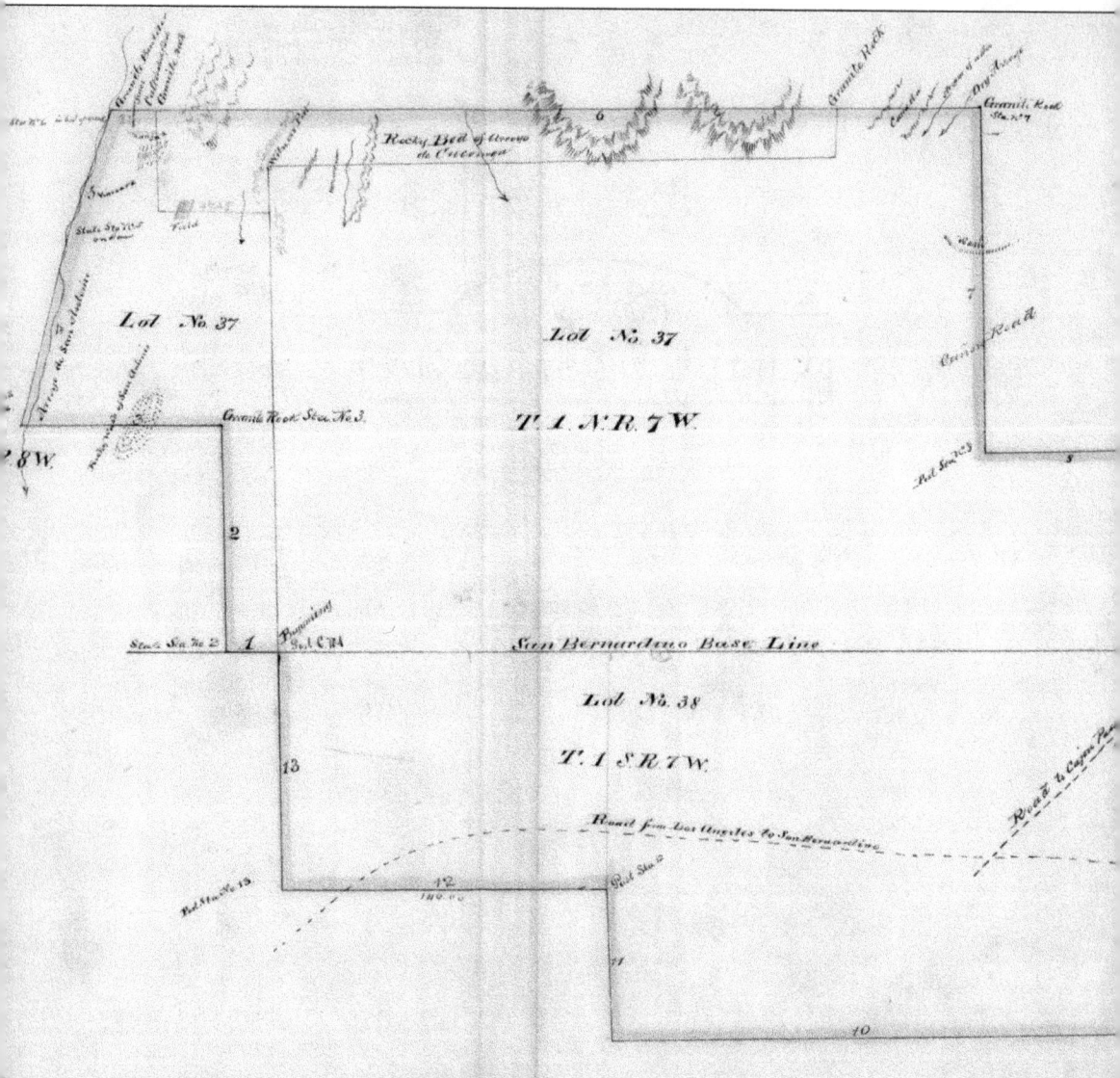

This 1865 survey map shows the borders of the Cucamonga Rancho that John and Maria Rains purchased from the heirs of Tiburcio Tapia. Today's city borders are very close to these original lines. Only two roads are shown here: the road from Los Angeles to San Bernardino, and the road to the Cajon Pass. The perfectly straight San Bernardino Base Line across the center was established by surveyors for measurement purposes. Today, it is the well-traveled Baseline Road. (Author's collection.)

ON THE COVER: The Atlantic Richfield station was one of first gas stations in Cucamonga, and it remains a noted landmark on Foothill Boulevard. It was built in 1914 and operated until 1972. The station remained abandoned for decades. The Route 66 Inland Empire California, a nonprofit group, began restoration of the station in 2013 to create a Route 66 museum. (Ed Dietl.)

IMAGES
of America

OLD CUCAMONGA

Paula Emick

ARCADIA
PUBLISHING

Copyright © 2015 by Paula Emick
ISBN 978-1-5316-7751-0

Published by Arcadia Publishing
Charleston, South Carolina

Library of Congress Control Number: 2014949899

For all general information, please contact Arcadia Publishing:
Telephone 843-853-2070
Fax 843-853-0044
E-mail sales@arcadiapublishing.com
For customer service and orders:
Toll-Free 1-888-313-2665

Visit us on the Internet at www.arcadiapublishing.com

To my ever-patient husband and family.

CONTENTS

ACKNOWLEDGMENTS

This book would not have been possible without the assistance of many wonderful people. The City of Rancho Cucamonga has been very supportive of both of my books. To the longtime residents who responded to notes and newspaper and Facebook announcements and came to Local History Night clutching your family history for me to scan, thank you. Thanks go to Elaine Craig, Linda Eddy, Pam Langmaack, Tim McCanless, Claudia Perdew, Maggie and Will Plunkett, and Karen Stanphil, for volunteering to share family photographs with the public.

Thank you, to Mary and Emily Blatnick, Sammy Dominick, Jackie Jeffers, Caroline Owens and Rosemary Owens, Al Scorsatto, Bill Yamaguchi, and Bob VanOosting, who each spent several hours sharing their photographs and stories. Special thanks go to the Filippi and Biane families, who have carried on their family legacies and preserved Cucamonga's wine history. You were very accommodating to my questions and requests. Kelly Zackman and the staff of the Ontario Model Colony History Room are always helpful in locating just the right picture for me.

Once again, I am indebted to Lucille Thompson and Shirley O'Morrow for the generous use of so many of the Stipe family photographs and for taking time to answer questions. Thanks go to Ed Dietl for his help and photographs—and for trying to understand my writing process. A big thank-you also goes to Marilyn Anderson of the Cooper Museum. You are so gracious to my last-minute questions and searches for information. I have learned a lot from you. I owe a huge debt of gratitude to a new history friend, Jane Vath O'Connell, who was a never-ending source of information and photographs, as well as a few laughs.

There is a special lady in the Northtown Community Center, Carol Norris, its board's president. When she is not helping the children and families of Northtown, she is working to preserve that community's history. She gave time from her extraordinarily busy schedule to assist me with this project. I wish her luck on her own book about Northtown.

Photographs without a credit line come from the author's collection. Photographs obtained from the Ontario Library's Robert E. Ellingwood Model Colony History Room are credited as "Ontario Library"; those from the Cooper Regional History Museum are credited as "Cooper Museum."

Lastly, a special thank-you goes to all the Rancho Cucamonga schoolteachers, including Dustin Guerra, who teach local history to their students so future generations will know the roots of this great city.

INTRODUCTION

Rancho Cucamonga's population has exploded since the three small towns of Etiwanda, Alta Loma, and Cucamonga incorporated into one city in 1977. What was it like before the land boom? In 1970, the population of Cucamonga was a mere 5,796 persons, and in 1950, it was just 1,255. Not everything and everyone in Cucamonga's history can be shown in one book. This small book of photographs is meant to give readers a "snapshot" of what life was like in Old Cucamonga.

Only the town of Cucamonga will be covered in this volume. Generally speaking, the borders of Cucamonga are roughly Baseline Road on the north, Vineyard Avenue on the west, Milliken Avenue on east, and Fourth Street on the south. Confusion can arise when looking at old documents, as the whole area including Ontario and east toward Riverside was called Cucamonga or the Cucamonga Wine Valley. Also, a winery could be referred to as the Cucamonga Winery, meaning it was a winery located in Cucamonga, or a winery called "Cucamonga Winery," whether or not that was its actual name. Add to that the fact that many wineries had "Cucamonga" in their official names. Research can become baffling. Then, there is the fact that North Cucamonga, or Northtown, is in the southern half of town. The area of South Cucamonga is in north Ontario. To clarify, Cucamonga Wine Valley extended south into present-day Ontario. That area is now called Guasti, named after the man who owned a very large vineyard and winery there in the 1900s. Back then, though, that area was called South Cucamonga. Many of its laborers lived in a community north of Guasti, hence North Cucamonga, or Northtown. Another large winery, the Padre Winery, also lay to the north of Guasti and was designated a North Cucamonga winery. Everyone understand?

The real history of Cucamonga begins long before the maps were drawn. The Los Angeles basin was home to Native Americans who called themselves the Tongva. Each tribe was an extended family unit of 20 to 100 people with its own name. Remnants of a Cucamonga village were found when Alta High School was built. The name refers both to the people and the land. Sometimes, the word is spelled "Kucomongo" or "Kucamonga" to differentiate it from modern Cucamonga. The suffix -nga, seen on many area names, means "place of" in Tongva. For instance, Tujunga means "old woman's place," as in Mother Earth. Temecula, a variation of Temeekunga, means "place of the sun." Pechanga means "place where the water drips," and Cucamonga means "place of many waters" or "sandy place."

Cucamonga's many waters came from the seasonal mountain streams that flood the land before sinking into the sandy soil of the valley floor. Flooding from the Cucamonga Creek over thousands of years brought rocks and sand down the hillsides and across the land. When the Spanish traveled through this area to colonize Alta California in the 1700s, they met the Kucomongo and discovered that the streams made an excellent rest stop after crossing the Mojave Desert.

The string of 21 California missions was operated by the Spanish from 1769 to 1833. For the pueblo of Los Angeles, there was the Mission San Gabriel Archangel, whose lands extended west and south to the Pacific Ocean and east to San Bernardino. The Tongva who were taken there to live were also called Gabrielino Indians. By the time the missions were closed by the newly established Mexican government, several generations of Tongva had lived away from their families' villages. Many of their descendants ended up living and working on the ranchos awarded to Mexican soldiers.

The story of modern-day Cucamonga begins with Tiburcio Tapia, a Mexican Army officer, businessman, smuggler, and politician in Los Angeles. In 1839, he was awarded 13,000 acres of land called Rancho Cucamonga by Mexico's governor, Juan Alvarado. Tapia planted a vineyard and raised cattle. On top of Red Hill, he built a fortress-like adobe home. A story is told that Tapia secretly buried a treasure chest of gold one night. Unfortunately, Tapia died suddenly a few days later. No one has ever admitted to finding the missing fortune. Perhaps it is still buried somewhere in Cucamonga.

It is said Tapia had a winery on his property beginning in 1838. There are conflicting reports and maps. Some say there was one, some say there was not. Historically, people believe the small adobe building attached to the bigger winery building was Tapia's winery. There was a vineyard (known today as the Thomas Winery), which meant Tapia made wine. Being a businessman, he probably sold wine. What is definitely known is that John Rains enlarged Tapia's vineyard, and sales of Cucamonga wine and grapes were documented. Works Progress Administration writers in 1933 said their research proved that the Cucamonga winery, now the Thomas winery, was the oldest commercial winery in California. In 1938, the people of Cucamonga started a new tradition to celebrate that distinction, the Wine and Grape Festival.

Wine is a huge part of Cucamonga's history. It brought the French, then the Italians. It brought investors, who made their fortunes elsewhere and wanted a quiet moneymaker for their golden years. It brought immigrants from China, Japan, and Mexico looking for work. There were over 60 wineries in the Cucamonga area as the years passed, and over 160 in Southern California. What was considered "wildland" became a mecca for those wanting a new start in life.

They built their lives one street and one neighborhood at a time along the stage routes to San Bernardino and Los Angeles, then along the railroad lines. As land was purchased, more streets were added. First, there was Archibald Avenue, which became Cucamonga's downtown for decades. Rock 'n' roll history would later be made there by renowned musician Frank Zappa. Fruit farmers came. Schools and churches were built and rebuilt. Businesses grew. Route 66 brought the world through the middle of the area. The wildland was tamed into a town.

The most remarkable thing about Cucamonga is its sense of community. Longtime residents, speaking with the author in person or through the Oral History Program, found on the city's Historic Preservation Program website, display a spirit of togetherness that helped them through difficult times. Neighbors helped neighbors. When illness or tragedy struck, neighbors and family came to a person's aid. In some neighborhoods in Cucamonga, the same families have lived there for over 100 years. Times could be very tough. But the ties between people seem to have been tougher. It is a lesson that people today could learn.

One

EARLY RESIDENTS OF THE CUCAMONGA RANCHO

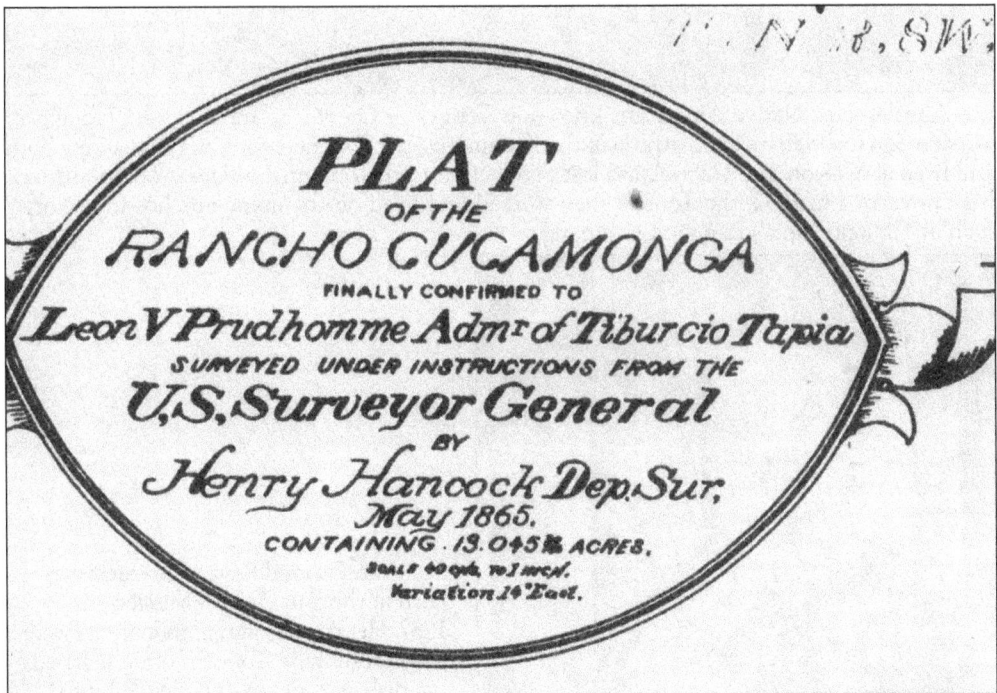

After Native Americans, Tiburcio Tapia was the first owner of the land that is now Rancho Cucamonga. This is the surveyor's seal of the map Tapias's heirs had drawn up for the sale of the Cucamonga Rancho to John Rains in 1865. It took several years for the deal to be finalized. The City of Rancho Cucamonga chose this traditional spelling when naming the city in 1977. But there were many spellings of the area's name, including Cocomungo, Cucamongabit, and Coco Mango. Cucamonga comes from the Tongva word meaning "place of many waters," referring to the springs and the many creeks running off the mountains.

Los Angeles–area Native Americans known as Tongva or Gabrielino Indians were brought to Mission San Gabriel, including those of the Kucamonga tribe. Generations of Tongva were born and lived at Mission San Gabriel and lost connection to their original villages. When missions were privatized in 1832, the Tongva then worked and lived on the many ranchos in the area, such as Tiburcio Tapia's Rancho Cucamonga.

Tongvan Pastoral Rosa Valenzuela was born at the San Gabriel Mission in 1887. Her parents and grandparents were Mission Indians. Tongvas often married Spanish Americans and blended into California society rather than return to traditional tribal life. Valenzuela was also a cousin of Doña Merced of the Chino Rancho, who purchased the Cucamonga Rancho with her husband, John Rains. Descendants of Valenzuela still live in Rancho Cucamonga. (Barbara Drake.)

One provision of the land grant made to Tiburcio Tapia in March 1839 was that he build a house and that it be inhabited. In addition to a fortress-like adobe home on top of Red Hill, there was another house near today's Thomas Winery. With a view looking west, the above photograph, taken in 1964, shows a repaired building that was intended to become a historic landmark. Unfortunately, the Old Homestead was destroyed in the 1969 flood. The 1938 Nash automobile advertisement, with a view looking east, shown below shows it in a very dilapidated state. The wood planks helped to cover and protect its adobe walls for 100 years. The area around the house would have been Tapia's vineyards, hence Vineyard Avenue. On the north side would be the dirt road that connected San Bernardino and Los Angeles, now San Bernardino Road. (Above, City of Rancho Cucamonga.)

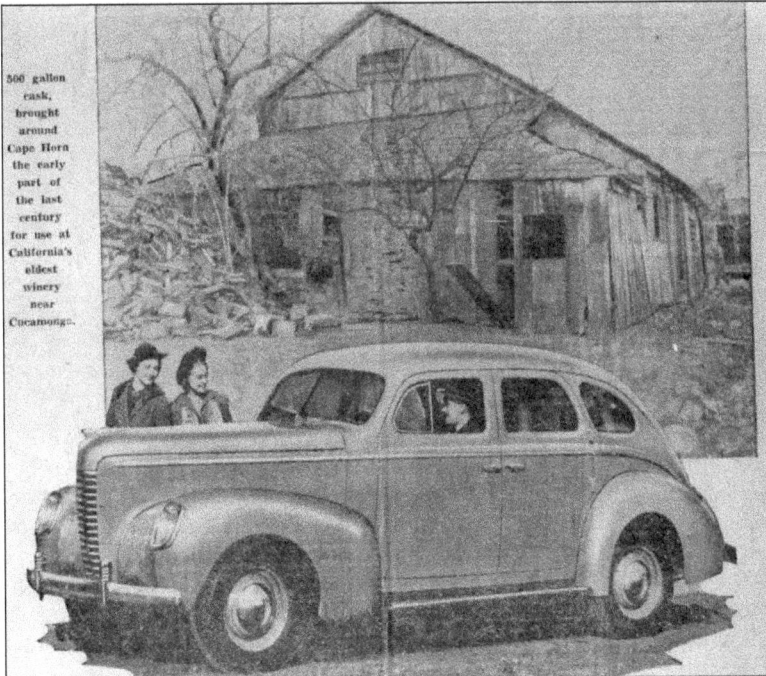

500 gallon cask, brought around Cape Horn the early part of the last century for use at California's oldest winery near Cucamonga.

Maria Merced Williams Rains, known as Doña Merced, was the daughter of Isaac Williams, one of California's richest cattle barons and owner of the Chino Rancho. A few days after her father's funeral, she married John Rains in 1856. She was just 17. When John was murdered in November 1862, rumors and threats alleged that Maria was involved with his death. Soldiers were posted at the rancho to protect her. In the end, no conclusive evidence was found to prosecute her. She remarried. Meanwhile, a combination of losses from droughts, heavy rains, and complications of business dealings resulted in Merced losing the Cucamonga Rancho to foreclosure. She moved to Los Angeles with her children. (Ontario Library.)

Some say that John Rains was an opportunist who swindled his wife out of her property and squandered her inheritance. He had worked as an Indian subagent on the Temecula property of his future father-in-law, Isaac Williams. At the time of his death, his credit was overextended and he had mortgaged the Cucamonga Rancho to finance investments, even though the property should have been in Merced's name. As he rode his horse to Los Angeles for business, Rains was ambushed and shot in Mud Springs (San Dimas). His killer was never found. It was suspected that Merced had hidden his pistols that morning, rendering him weaponless on the day of his murder, but this was never proven. (Ontario Library.)

The John Rains House was the first fired-brick building in San Bernardino County. The red clay for the bricks came from the once marshy area southwest of Red Hill. Its front room served as the area's first school, making it the original building for the Cucamonga School District. The house, located on the corner of Vineyard Avenue and Hemlock Street, is now a museum site.

A unique feature of the Rains House is a water flume that ran underneath it. Water was diverted from a nearby spring to a small reservoir. From there, the water flowed under the kitchen, through the center courtyard, and under the front bedroom. There was no need to haul water from a well, and this feature helped keep the house cool in the scorching summer heat.

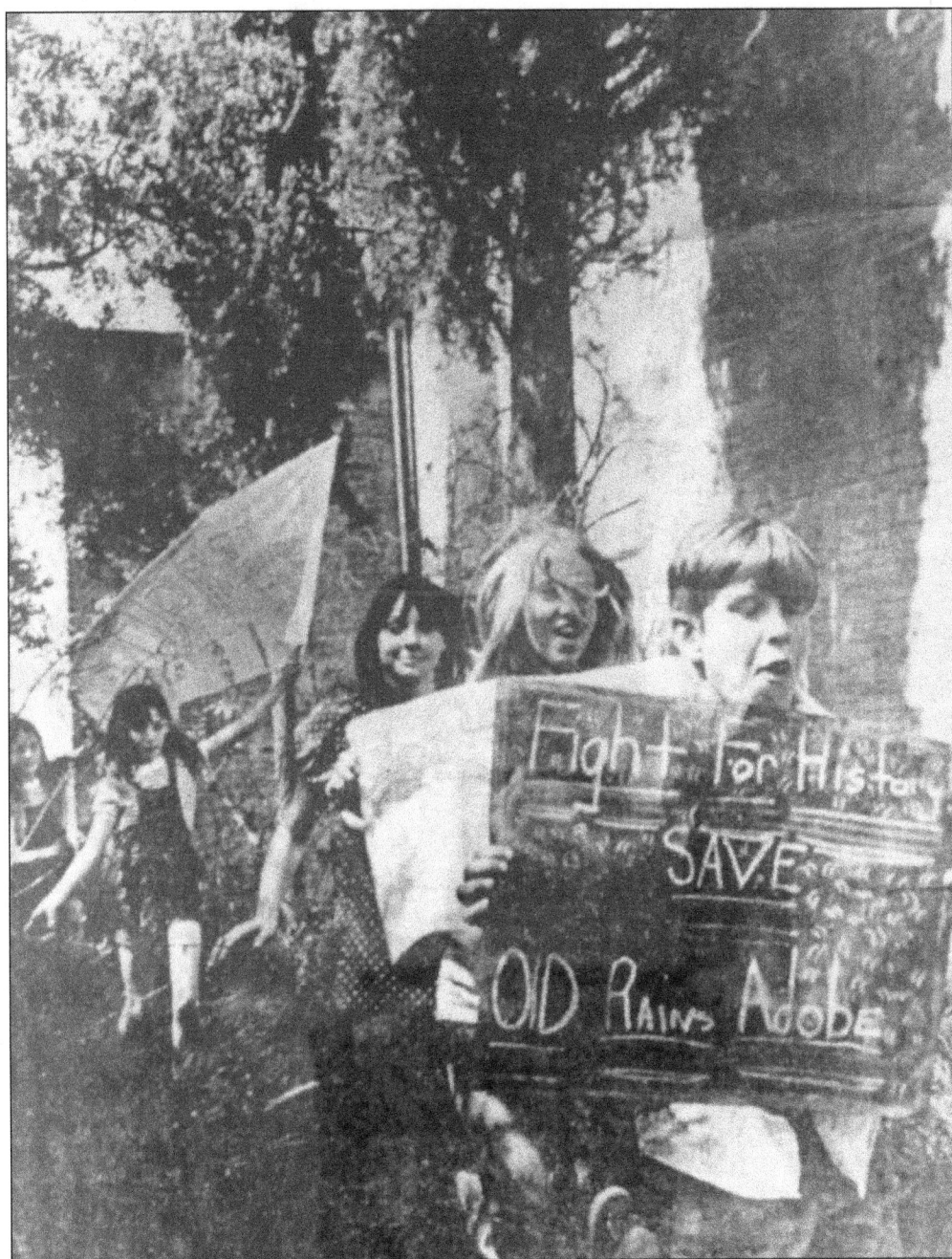

On June 1, 1971, schoolchildren and their teacher held a protest march demanding to save the historic Rains House from destruction. On a recent field trip with their teacher, Maxine Strane, the students had come across a bulldozer poised to knock down the vacant building to make room for more tract houses. Leaving the students and another teacher to stand guard, Strane ran back to the school to make phone calls to delay the demolition. Over the following days, she enlisted students for the protest and to help clean up the grounds. In the end, the San Bernardino County Museum purchased the property. Cucamonga's landmark was saved. Over the years, volunteers have beautifully restored the house.

William Rubottom, known as "Uncle Billy," is remembered for several reasons. For one, he built and operated the Mountain View Inn at the Butterfield stagecoach stop in Cucamonga. Also, in the tavern of that inn, Rubottom is credited with saving the life of Doña Merced from a group of vigilantes who blamed her for her husband's murder. It is said that Rubottom overheard the dozen men planning to lynch Merced as they ate supper. Rubottom and his son held them at gunpoint and sent the mob home with instructions to return separately for their guns on another day. Lastly, a local story says that Uncle Billy is the reason opossums, which are indigenous to the eastern and midwestern United States, are in California. It is said that Rubottom brought opossums from Arkansas to make his famous possum stew for the customers of his inn. Possibly, he brought them to provide game for local hunters. Most likely, Rubottom was not the only settler to bring opossums to the West Coast. In any case, opossums have populated California ever since. (Ontario Library.)

16

It was a two-day stagecoach ride from Los Angeles to the big, bustling citrus town of San Bernardino. Cucamonga is about halfway between the two cities. Like the owners of gas stations and hotels decades later along Route 66, Billy Rubottom saw a business opportunity. He already owned a stage stop in Spadra, now Pomona. He purchased land and built a second Butterfield stagecoach stop in Cucamonga. Twice a day, mail and passengers stopped at the Mountain View Inn. Eventually, the inn burned down, and the stage was replaced by trains and automobiles. John Klusman bought the property and built the Sycamore Inn, which still stands today.

Chinese laborers return from the vineyards to the Cucamonga (Thomas) Winery in a painting based on a c. 1900 photograph. Many of the Chinese who labored on the Transcontinental Railroad later came to Southern California to work in vineyards and orchards. Others worked at digging the water tunnels through the mountains north of Upland. The majority of these workers eventually returned to their families and homeland. (Painting by the author.)

Cucamonga's Chinatown house is located on San Bernardino Road and Klusman Avenue. The first Chinatown was a group of wooden shacks that burned down. The Araiza family owned the land and erected this brick building to replace what fire had destroyed. This building is one of the last remaining structures used by the Chinese in early California history.

Two

BUILDING CUCAMONGA

After the foreclosure of Cucamonga Rancho, its land was bought and subdivided, sold and resold. Farmers, ranchers, blacksmiths, bankers, and store owners came to Cucamonga to make a living. The Cucamonga Hall was located on the east side of Archibald Avenue, just north of present-day Foothill Boulevard. A dry-goods store downstairs supplied the town's residents with any number of items, from coffee and flour, to fabric and dishes, to tools and hardware. Farmers could order seeds and other items from catalogs and have them delivered to the store by stage or train. Early store owners Loyal and Goe Streiby are pictured. (City of Rancho Cucamonga.)

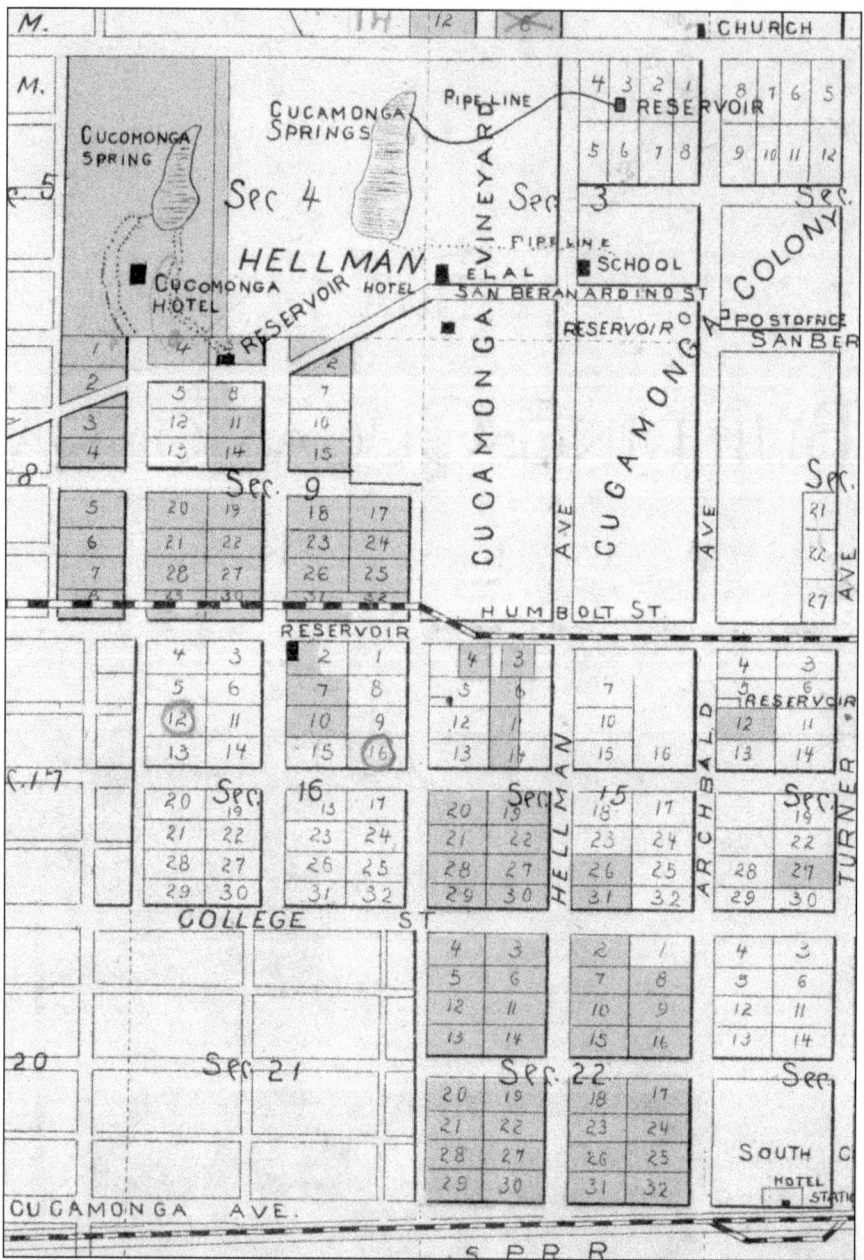

Many streets are named after early Cucamonga landowners. Hellman Avenue is named for Isaias Hellman, who purchased much of the foreclosed rancho property. Some land he held directly, and some via his Cucamonga Homestead Association. Another landowner was John Archibald (or Archbald). There is debate as to whether the map shows a printing error, or if the name there, Archbald, is the correct spelling. Nevertheless, Archibald Avenue became the center of town. Note that the map shows no Foothill Boulevard. What will later become the "Stone or Rock Church" is still a wooden building on Baseline Road. The Cucamonga School is on San Bernardino Road. The post office has already been moved from the stagecoach stop by the Rains House to Archibald Avenue, possibly in the Cucamonga Hall. An unnamed building near Vineyard Avenue is most likely the Cucamonga/Thomas Winery or the Old Homestead adobe. (Ontario Library.)

20

CHURCH   T. I. N. R. I W.   T. I. N.

HERMOSA   AVE

VOIR 8 7 6 5 | 4 3 2 1 | 8 7 6 5 | 4 3 2 1

9 10 11 12 | 13 14 15 16 | 9 10 | 31 32

12 11 | 30 29

Sec. 2   17 | 13 Sec | 27 28

COLONY   18 | 16 15 | 26 25

POSTOFFICE   19 20 | 17 18 19 20 | 21 22 23 24

SAN BERNARDINO ST.

3 2 1

13 14 15 16

Sec. 11   HAVEN   AND

21   MILLIKEN

22   VINEYARD

27

NORTH CUCAMONGA   A.T. & S.F.R.R

4 3   DEPOT
5 6
RESERVOIR
12 11
13 14

TURNER   Sec. 14   Sec. 13
19 18 17 | 20 19 | 18 17
22 23 24 | 21 22 | 23 24
28 27 26 25 | 28 27 | 26 25
29 30 31 32 | 29 30 | 31 32

HAVEN

4 3 2 1 | 4 3 2 1
5 6 7 8 | 5 6 7 8
12 11 10 9 | 12 11 10 9
13 14 13 16 | 13 14 15 16

Sec. 23   Sec. 24
20 19 | 18 17
21 22 | 23 24
SOUTH CUCAMONGA   28 27 | 26 25
HOTEL   29 30 | 31 32
STATION

S P R R

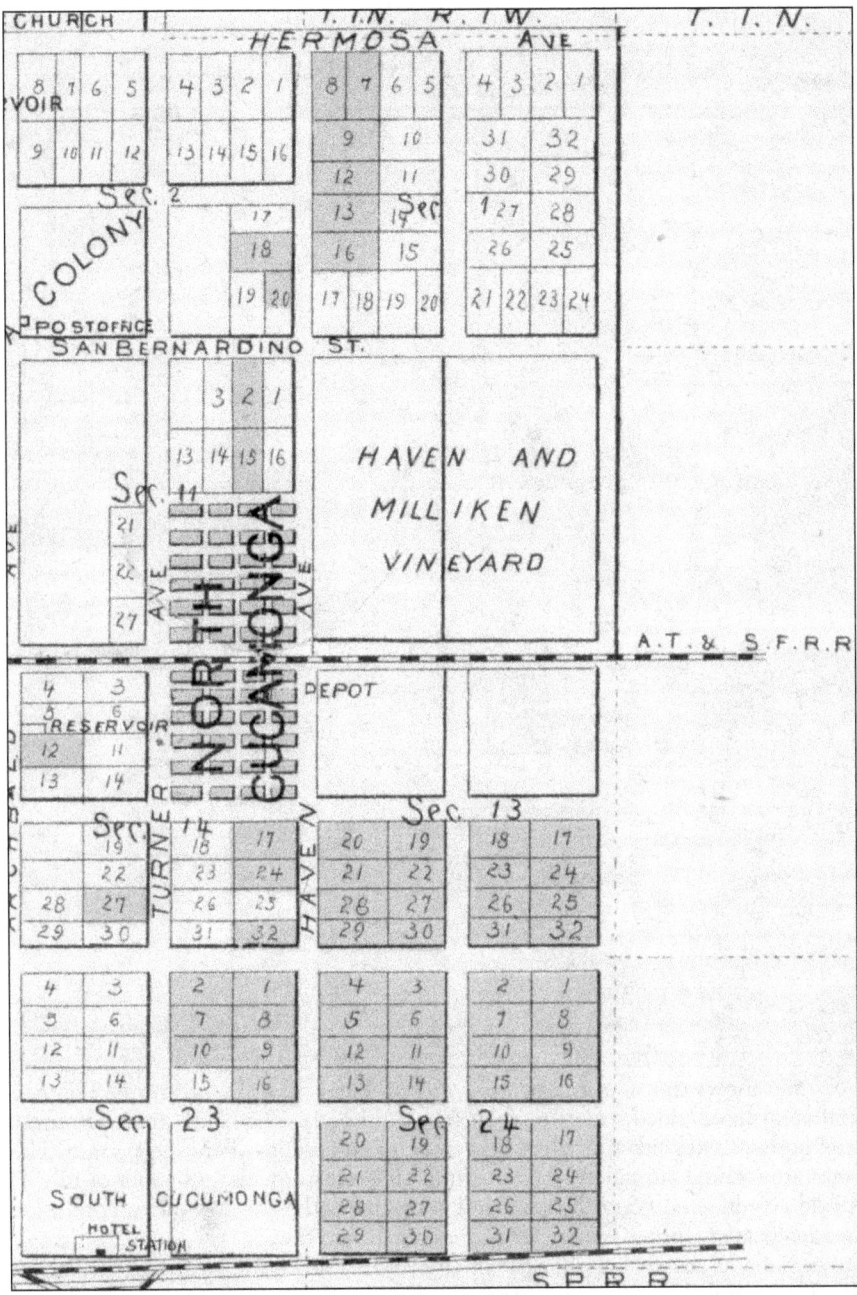

The east side of this 1870s map shows an area labeled "North Cucamonga." It was so named for being north of the Southern Pacific train station and the Guasti Winery in South Cucamonga, now part of Ontario. North Cucamonga became known as Northtown. Its residents worked at the Santa Fe Railway depot, local ranches, and the packinghouses on Eighth Street. Haven and Milliken Avenues were named after George Haven and Daniel Milliken, prominent dry ranchers who raised grapes without irrigation. At the map's top, Hermosa Avenue runs east-west as a section of Baseline Road. Later, Turner Avenue would be renamed Hermosa Avenue, except for a short bit south of Fourth Street. Reservoirs were located throughout town to supply water to homes and farms. (Ontario Library.)

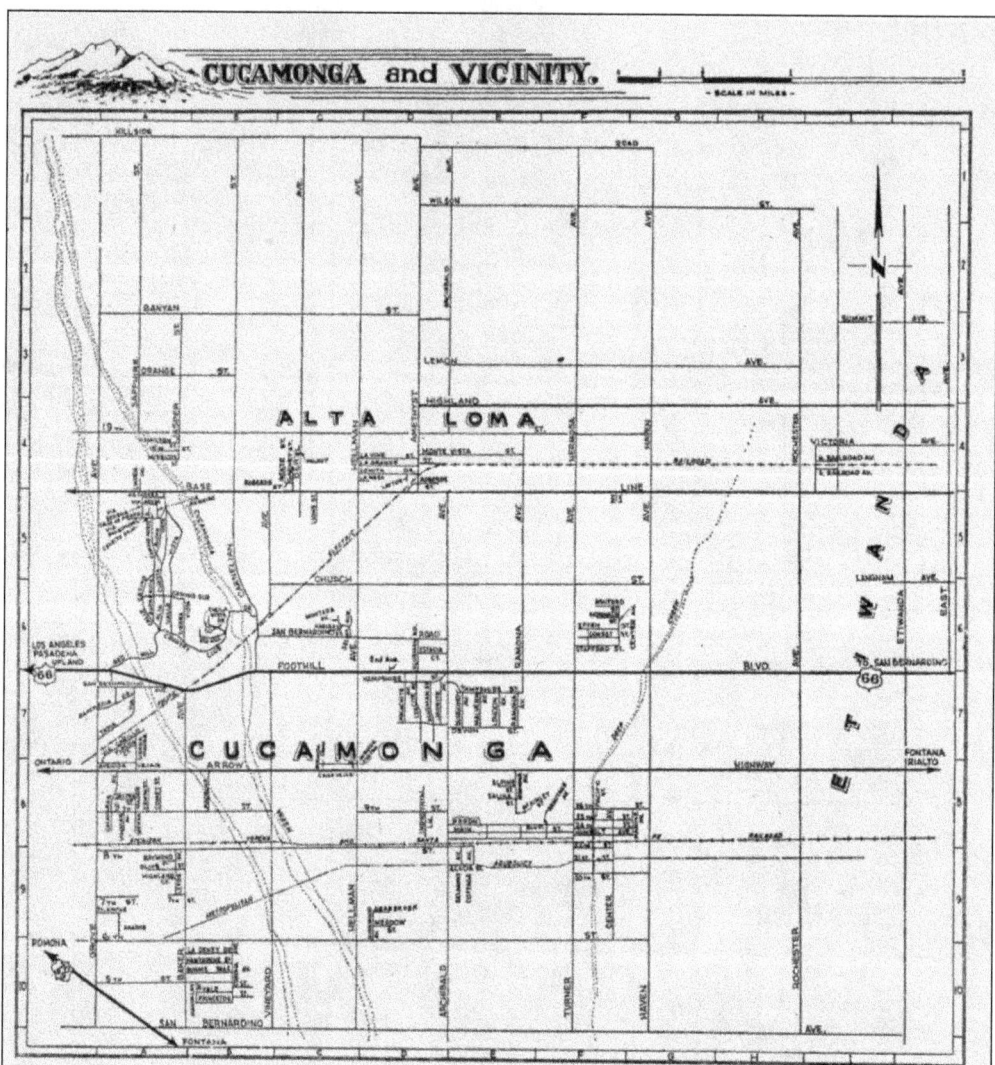

CUCAMONGA and VICINITY.

This 1962 map shows that Cucamonga has grown, but it is still quite rural. The pockets of residential areas have added streets to their neighborhoods. The blank areas surrounding the small neighborhoods are citrus ranches, vineyards, or empty lots where sheep graze. The creeks and washes are marked, as widespread flooding after rainstorms is still a fact of life. The area of Archibald Avenue and Foothill Boulevard continues to be the downtown core, where most businesses are located. Turner Avenue continues northward toward Alta Loma. Milliken Avenue has yet to be built, as the area is still acres of vineyards. The Pacific Electric Railroad, known as the Red Car line, is labeled, although passenger service had been discontinued with the expansion of the freeway system. (Caroline Owen.)

"WELCOME TO THE LAND OF OPPORTUNITY"

Cucamonga District Chamber of Commerce

P. O. Box 236 YUkon 2-3012
9334 San Bernardino Road
Cucamonga, California

———o———

IN CASE OF FIRE CALL —

CUCAMONGA . . .	2-1102
ALTA LOMA . . .	2-1105
ETIWANDA . .	Etiwanda 6373

———o———

LAW ENFORCEMENT SERVICES

SHERIFF'S DEPT. .	Yukon 4-2731 or Etiwanda 6161
HIGHWAY PATROL	ZEnith 1-2000
CONSTABLE—CUCAMONGA and ALTA LOMA	YUkon 2-8891
CONSTABLE— ETIWANDA .	Etiwanda 6331

———o———

UTILITY SERVICES

Cucamonga Water District	Yu. 2-6096
Southwest Water Co.	Etiwanda 6555
General Telephone Co.	Yukon 6-3841
Southern California Gas Company . .	Zenith 5851
Southern California Edison Company .	Yukon 6-5861
for Etiwanda .	Zenith 2-1300

The map's key, shown here, provides some interesting information about Cucamonga in the early 1960s. The chamber of commerce's slogan, "Welcome to the Land of Opportunity," reflects the era's positive outlook. Each town had its own fire department, and local police were referred to with the gentler term *constable*. Note that phone numbers are five digits, preceded by two letters identifying the telephone exchange. Since letters can sound very similar, words were used to help people differentiate. This is why the number keys on a phone have letters on them. The prefix Yukon represented 98, Zenith stood for 93. By the late 1960s, the letters were dropped, and seven-digit phone numbers became the norm. (Caroline Owens.)

Daniel Milliken made his money in lumber before moving to Cucamonga in 1883 to try something new. He partnered with George Haven and invested in a grand experiment called dry ranching. They purchased over 500 acres of wild desert and planted grapes without irrigation. They were called fools for planting in dry ground. Opinions changed when the grapes took root and thrived in the sandy soil.

Except for the paved street, this 1978 north-facing view of Haven Avenue near Foothill Boulevard shows a scene not much different from that facing George Haven when he arrived in Cucamonga in 1881, after making his fortune in mining. The success of dry ranching inspired other grape growers, such as Secondo Guasti, to plant and expand. Haven later organized the Cucamonga Vintage Company to help growers secure fairs prices for their harvests. (Maggie and Will Plunkett.)

24

Built in 1928, the George Klusman House stands on Foothill Boulevard west of Vineyard Avenue. George Klusman and his three brothers—William, Henry, and John—emigrated from Germany and made their livelihoods in Cucamonga. George farmed potatoes, in addition to grapes and other crops, on the surrounding land. The structure is still used as a home and a business location. (Ed Dietl.)

Henry "Hank" Klusman arrived in 1891 from Germany and initially worked on his brother William's farm to repay his travel expenses. Henry's construction company built most of Cucamonga's business district, the Chaffey Library, the stone Methodist church, numerous grammar schools, and many other buildings. Later, he specialized in irrigation pipe. He is shown here working on a project in 1956. (United Methodist Church of Cucamonga.)

The essentials of a downtown are shown in this south-facing view of Archibald Avenue in the early 1900s. The first building on the right houses a barbershop, a store, and the Cucamonga Post Office. Behind the telephone pole is the brick bank building that would one day house the *Cucamonga Times*. At center, behind the tree, is San Bernardino Road. Beyond that is a Williams-Lucas store. Lucas owned a large ranch and other properties. (Jane Vath O'Connell.)

In this north-facing view of Archibald Avenue in the 1930s, the number of parked cars suggests that one of the men's service clubs is having a meeting, with breakfast cooked by the members' wives. In a small town, volunteer service groups were essential for taking care of the community, whether it was helping the needy, improving the roads, or organizing social events, such as the Grape and Wine Festival. (Brancacio-Owen family.)

Rock 'n' roll history was made on Archibald Avenue in the early 1960s. A young Frank Zappa (right), who would one day became a music icon, teamed up with Paul Bluff, another musician, and opened PAL Recording Studio, first at 8020 Archibald Avenue, then at no. 8040, to the right Paul's Shoes. Zappa renamed it Studio Z after Bluff left for another production opportunity. In late 1962, a teenage band from Glendora named the Surfaris came to record a song. The Surfaris were packing up their gear when Zappa asked about their B side. The teens replied that they did not have one. Within the hour, with Zappa's help, they had arranged and recorded what would become one of the most memorable surf tunes of all time, "Wipeout." Zappa later recorded an album entitled *Cucamonga*. (Right, Wikimedia Commons; below, Cooper Museum.)

This brick building, on the northwest corner of Archibald Avenue and San Bernardino Road, housed a branch of the First National Bank of Cucamonga. Interestingly, the bank was established in San Bernardino. When the bank closed in the 1930s, the *Cucamonga Times* newspaper office moved in. For more than six decades, the paper came out once a week, on Thursday, featuring both the big and small news stories of the area. (Brancacio-Owen family.)

Leslie "Scoop" Foster (left) was not the first editor of the *Cucamonga Times*, but he was perhaps the most memorable. With a pipe clenched in his teeth, he worked seven days a week selling advertisements, typing articles, and setting type on the ancient printing press. His folksy front-page column began with the reminder "the finest thing about Cucamonga is all the nice folks who live here." (Elaine Craig.)

The *Cucamonga Times* began reporting the town's news in 1909. When the printer in Pomona bought a new press, the *Times* was given the old one. This ancient press was used for several more decades before being replaced. Silas Craig, who ran a printing press in the Times Building and took over as editor in 1965, sits at the 19th-century press. The small-town paper was published until the mid-1970s. (Elaine Craig.)

The First National Bank of Cucamonga opened in 1904 and printed paper money until 1934. In the nation's early years, banks printed money. By 1861, thousands of bills in different sizes, designs, colors, and denominations were in circulation. Counterfeit currency was a major problem. The National Banks Acts of 1863 and 1864 ruled that banks could only produce notes on paper authorized by the US government, using the same basic artwork and design. The Cucamonga $10 bill shown above reflects that rule. In 1929, the federal government further regulated currency by reducing the size and determining the appearance of bills. The Federal Bureau of Printing and Engraving then took over the task of printing money. Banks had to dismantle their printing presses. The stock certificate shown below belonged to James Vai, one the Padre Winery's first owners. (Below, Biane family.)

MAIN OFFICE
LOS ANGELES DIVISION
SEVENTH STREET AT OLIVE

16·66   16·66

LOS ANGELE

Bank of Italy
NATIONAL TRUST & SAVINGS ASSOCIATION

PAY

ITALI
VINEY.

JANUARY

BASILIO MARTINEZ   #13

Guasti, California

The Bank of Italy, founded in San Francisco in 1904, was established to serve the Italian American working class in Northern California. By 1918, the bank had 24 branches and was the first statewide branch-banking system. The Bank of Italy was used by the many Italians in the Cucamonga and Los Angeles areas working in the wine industry. In 1928, the bank expanded by merging with the smaller Bank of America in Los Angeles. The Bank of Italy changed its name to Bank of America two years later for a wider commercial appeal. This 1930 paycheck from the Italian Vineyard Company was issued shortly before the bank changed its name. (Biane family.)

In March 1864, Pres. Abraham Lincoln established the post office in Cucamonga, the first in the West End of San Bernardino County. This house served as the first Cucamonga Post Office. It stood on the east side of Vineyard Avenue, across from the Rains House on the San Bernardino Road stagecoach route. Jeffrey W. Gillette, the first postmaster, collected $16.24 a year for his service. (Mary Blatnick.)

For 54 years, residents would pick up their mail once a week at the post office, until rural delivery service was started locally in 1918. City delivery began in 1956. The location of the post office changed at least four times before 1966. Here, postmaster Anton Blatnick stands in front of the post office's longtime location on Archibald Avenue, across from the offices of the *Cucamonga Times*. (Mary Blatnick.)

Dedication

of the

New United States Post Office
Cucamonga, California 91730

Saturday, September 17, 1966

3:00 o'clock

Sponsored by

Cucamonga District Chamber of Commerce

In 1966, a new postal facility was built on Klusman Avenue. Months earlier, the ground was broken with a golden spade by Miss Cucamonga, Sherry Fuches. At the building's dedication, dignitaries were present and speeches were made. Refreshments were served afterwards by the wives of the employees. Within 20 years, this location was outgrown, and the post office moved to its present location on Arrow Highway. (Mary Blatnick.)

The United Methodist Church of Cucamonga, also known as the Old Stone or Rock Church, on the corner of Church Street and Archibald Avenue, began as a wooden building on Baseline Road, but the fierce winds knocked it down. A second building also succumbed to wind. In 1909, a solidly built church was constructed under Henry Klusman's supervision, using volunteer labor and 373 wagonloads of rock brought from the canyons. (United Methodist Church of Cucamonga.)

A bagpiper gets ready to play for a wedding. Churches were not just for weddings and baptisms. They served as centers of the community. Socials and dinners at churches provided entertainment for the townspeople. In the early years, when not every family had a car to get to the local theater in Upland, the Methodist church rented a movie weekly to show on the wall of the fellowship room. (United Methodist Church of Cucamonga.)

Above, children color and write at Vacation Bible School with their teacher in the 1970s. Many families rely on churches for religious instruction for their children as well as for fun activities. Below, children excitedly search for eggs in an outdoor Easter egg hunt in the field north of the church as parents look on in the 1950s. (Both, United Methodist Church of Cucamonga.)

The Cucamonga School, seen above, was built in the late 1800s on the corner of Hellman Avenue and San Bernardino Road. Below, children in the early 1900s sit on the west side of the school for their class photograph. By 1912, a larger school was needed; it was planned to be built in Northtown. But parents near Foothill Boulevard wanted to keep the closer location. Neither side would compromise. The district split in two. In 1915, the Central Cucamonga District, later the Central School District, opened with a new school on the San Bernardino Road location. In 1916, a new Cucamonga School building was opened on Archibald Avenue at Eighth Street. (Above, City of Rancho Cucamonga; below, Central School District.)

Henry Klusman's construction company replaced the wooden schoolhouse in 1915 with a larger, Mission-style school, the construction of which is shown here. This design was common in Southern California. Klusman built most of the Archibald Avenue business district and the Chaffey Memorial Library, as well as grammar schools in Barstow, Needles, Alta Loma, Twentynine Palms, and, of course, Cucamonga. Klusman is pictured in the lower right, wearing a suit and cap. (Jackie Cartwright Jeffers.)

Grades first through eighth were taught in the Cucamonga School, with two grades per classroom. When this building became too small in the 1940s, a new Central Elementary School was built on Archibald Avenue. This building then became Sweeten Hall, named after Ray Sweeten, editor of the *Cucamonga Times*, who left $1,000 in his will to start a recreation center for the town. The building continues to serve the public today. (Jackie Cartwright Jeffers.)

Behind Cucamonga School was a baseball field that was used by all the teams in town. Here, the Hoyt Lumber team poses in 1934. Players are, from left to right, Dale Pittinger, Jimmy Watson, Arval Smith, Russ Patanae, Harold Davis, Jim Wattenburger, Babe Slow, Lewis Davis, Garland Smith, Howard Wikes, Floyd Wattenburger, Carl Mathis, and Frank Baine. The coaches at either end are unidentified. (Shirley O'Morrow.)

Cucamonga Central School's seventh and eighth grade class of 1928–1929 is seen here along with the teacher. Pictured are, from left to right, (first row) Leva Arnold, Magdalena Campanella, Josephine Emery, Letty Lundeen, Bessie Duncan, Myrtle Minor, Lucille Stipe, and Hazel Spangler; (second row) Forest Wattenburger, David McCorkle, Billy Owings, Jimmy Gregorio, and Milton Thompson; (third row) Joan Lopez, Maureen Chappell, Margaret Klusman, and Orsolina Campanella; (fourth row) Jack Whitney, Cleo Oakley, Mable Cooper (teacher), George Klusman Jr., Philip List, and ? Yee. (Lucille Thompson.)

The Cucamonga Fire Department on San Bernardino Road near Klusman Avenue began as a small two-bay station. Cucamonga organized its own volunteer fire department in 1947 to answer calls that had been directed to Upland and the US Forest Service. Above, the fire engines parked in front of the station are a 1954 GMC Yankee (left) and a 1948 Ford General. Below, the same station is pictured today, after being enlarged and given a face-lift in the Mission Revival style. There are plans to replace this station in the future. (Above, City of Rancho Cucamonga.)

Almost anything could be ordered from the Sears, Roebuck and Co. catalog—even a house. Customers had several models to choose from. Precut lumber, doors, windows, and all the required hardware would be shipped by train. The homeowners could assemble the house themselves or hire a local contractor to do it for them. (Ed Dietl.)

The Emery House, at 7403 Archibald Avenue, was part of a 10-acre citrus ranch that included its own sorting and packing barn. Its orange groves were maintained until the 1970s. A Sears catalog with the house-plans page marked was found in the attic. Historians believe this may be a Sears kit house, or at least copied after one. (Ed Dietl.)

The Christmas House, on 9240 Archibald Avenue, was built by H.D. Cousins in 1904. Its nickname comes from its red-and-green stained-glass windows and the festive parties held by the Whitsons, the home's owners from 1910 to 1970. Today, it is a bed-and-breakfast. (Ed Dietl.)

The Cucamonga Public Market, built by Henry Klusman on the southeast corner of Archibald Avenue and Foothill Boulevard, is one of the few early buildings in town that not only is still standing, but is still operating in much the same way as it started. For the last few decades, it has been known as the home of Carl's Liquor and the Deli sandwich shop. (Brancacio-Owen family.)

The outline of the building has remained the same over the decades. Years earlier, the coffee shop on the end was Lucy and John's. It later moved down the street and eventually became the Magic Lamp. Another well-known restaurant, Socorro's, also got its start here. (Brancacio-Owen family.)

This 1940s photograph shows that the Hot Lunches place has been upgraded to a café. In the center, squeezed in between the café and Archibald Avenue, is a small Union 76 gas station. Across the street is Ray Ford's Texaco station, where a Bank of America now stands. Foothill Boulevard was a two-lane highway at this time, with plenty of room for parking in front of businesses. (Sammy Dominick.)

In 1957, Carl and Margaret Brancacio made the switch from renting the store space to owning the building. Their landlord envied the Brancacios' nearby peach orchard property. So, a trade was made: one building for one orchard. Carl's Liquor Store is still in business. The peach orchard site became a new tract of homes. Years later, the Brancacios opened the Deli, a popular sandwich shop, on the west end of the building. (Brancacio-Owen family.)

With a view looking east on Foothill Boulevard/Route 66 from Archibald Avenue, this photograph is from the 1940s. (Sammy Dominick.)

In this view looking north up Vineyard Avenue by Candlewood Street in February 1978, the future Red Hill Park is seen on the left. At this point, the land was still a catch basin for storm runoff, with native scrub brush growing in and around it. John Rains and later Rains House owners used this area as a water reservoir. (Maggie and Will Plunkett.)

The Dominicks work in their yard along a peaceful Highway 66 in this photograph, taken around 1945, with a west-facing view of Foothill Boulevard. This is a couple doors west of Dee's Diner, across the street from the Cucamonga Market. An undeveloped Red Hill is in the background. There were no traffic signals in Cucamonga yet; cars were to slow to 25 miles per hour when coming into a town. (Sammy Dominick.)

The Bank of America, once the Bank of Italy, and Vath's Cucamonga Drugstore grace this 1955 postcard. Beautiful snow covers Cucamonga Peak in the background. Like many old-time drugstores, Vath's had an ice-cream counter and a soda fountain. (Jane Vath O'Connell.)

Clerk Susie Hamner (center) assists shopper Luella Wangler in the brand-new Vath's Cucamonga Drugstore on Archibald Avenue. There were no 24-hour pharmacies then. In a small community, if customers needed medicine after-hours, they could call the pharmacist at home. He would then open the store and fill their prescriptions. (Jane Vath O'Connell.)

46

KEEPING PACE WITH CUCAMONGA'S GROWTH

VISIT OUR BEAUTIFUL NEW STORE

A complete family drug store selling only the finest products marketed today. You will find every need supplied by modern day drug stores at Cucamonga Drug. Medicinal products covering many branches to be sure . . . but also the finest in cosmetics, a greeting card department, photographic needs and service, candies, and all the other departments necessary to making up a fine drug store.

Cucamonga Drugs specializes in prescriptions taking great pride and care in compounding the prescription you bring from your doctor.

With others of this community, we take pride in congratulating the creators and builders of Cucamonga's beautiful new medical center.

TED VATH, Prop.

CUCAMONGA DRUG

8069 Archibald Ave., Cucamonga   **YU. 2-1509**

In 1958, Vath's Cucamonga Drugstore moved around the corner to Archibald Avenue and into a brand-new, modern building constructed by Henry Klusman. This drugstore was the first in town to carry name-brand cosmetics. Vath's daughter remarked, "It went from dime store to Max Factor overnight." Ted Vath owned two other drugstores as well—one in Alta Loma, and the other in Grand Terrace. Vath sold the two local Cucamonga Drugstores to Gemmel, another family-owned drugstore chain. He kept the third as a "hobby" after he retired. (Jane Vath O'Connell.)

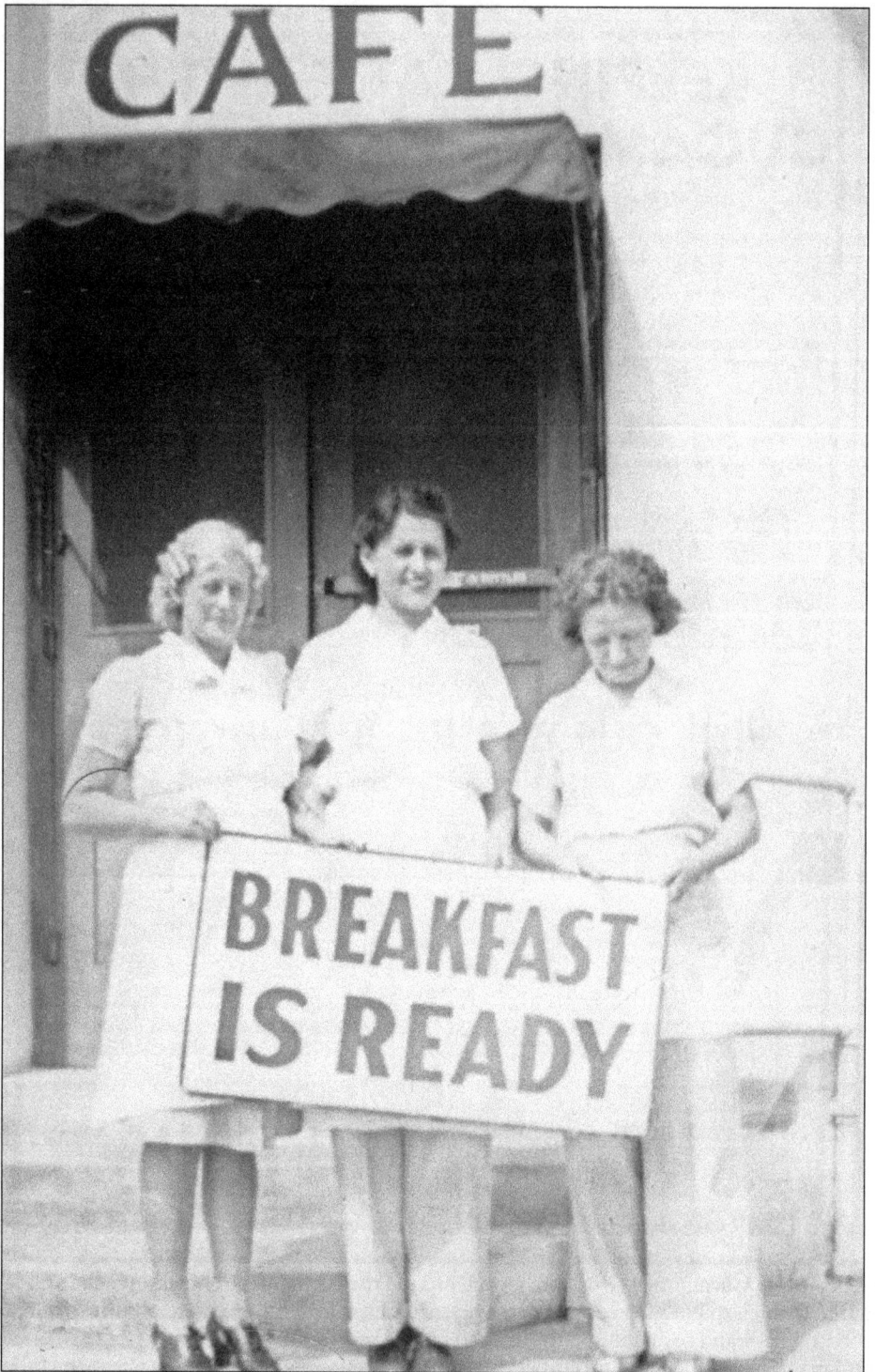

Breakfast is ready at the Old Cucamonga Café in 1945. First owned in the 1930s by members of the Frost family, the café was purchased by the Dominicks in 1945. It was located on Highway 66, Foothill Boulevard, east of Archibald Avenue. (Sammy Dominick.)

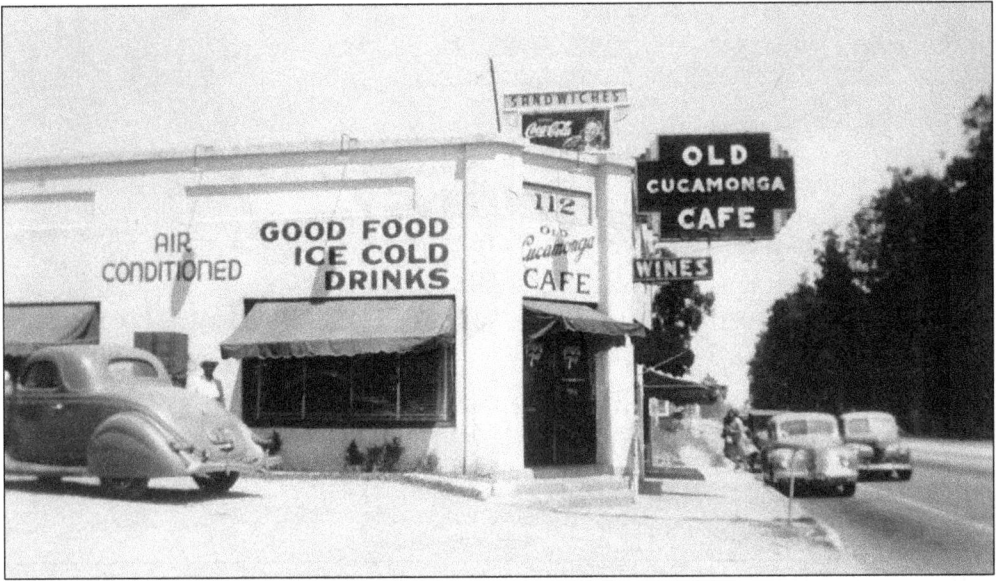

The Old Cucamonga Café, on the north side of Highway 66, was about a block east of Archibald Avenue. An air-conditioned place to stop and eat on a hot summer's day was enticing in a time when many cars and houses did not have such a luxury. Below, a jukebox stands ready to play the top tunes for a nickel. Owners Nora and Sam Dominick are behind the counter, ready to serve their customers in the late 1940s. (Both, Sammy Dominick.)

ON THE STRIP
CUCAMONGA : CALIFORNIA

PRESENTS

Elegant Ethyl

Playing her tintillating tunes each Sunday after-
noon, Tuesday, Thursday, Friday a n d Saturday
evening from 7:30 'til those hours decreed by our
esteemed Alcoholic Beverage Control Board in
this roaring year of Our Lord, 1959.

After the Old Cucamonga Café closed, it became a number of bar-and-grill establishments. A well-known one was Shanty Devlin's. Elegant Ethyl knew all the songs. She played the piano and sang for $15 and a beer. Ethel Fernbach passed away in July 1964 after a sudden illness. (Jane Vath O'Connell.)

This section of Foothill Boulevard is about a block east of Archibald Avenue. The Shanty bar and grill (left) operated under several different owners, as evidenced in old photographs. Huge shopping malls and chain restaurants were getting their start elsewhere in metropolitan areas. But rural places such as Cucamonga relied on mom-and-pop places for entertainment and food.

RED HILL COUNTRY CLUB, ONTARIO, CALIF.
5626

For more sophisticated dining and entertainment, there was the Red Hill Country Club, which opened on March 18, 1922, with a nine-hole golf course. The second nine holes were added in 1946. Memberships originally sold for $220, with dues of $5 per month. Over the years, the clubhouse and grounds have been rebuilt several times. Note that this postcard lists the city as Ontario. Red Hill sits next to the border of Upland and Rancho Cucamonga. At one time, that strip of land was part of Upland, which was originally called North Ontario. (Jane Vath O'Connell.)

We have received the plaudits of diners from coast to coast. They all tell us how much they enjoy the individuality and delicious flavoring of Cafe Italiano's excellent dishes. We specialize in Italian - American foods. Being located in Cucamonga at Archibald Ave. and Foothill Blvd., Cafe Italiano can conveniently fit your scheme for dining out. Visit Us Today!

The Italian influence from the age of wineries continued in the area for many years. The Café Italiano, on the northwest corner of Archibald Avenue and Foothill Boulevard, was a favored restaurant in Cucamonga known for its elegance and wonderful food. Most Cucamonga restaurants could be found on Foothill Boulevard (Route 66). Unfortunately, the restaurant was destroyed in a fire and was never rebuilt. (Below, Brancacio-Owen family.)

The Fry family built a diner by converting a bus, like the one pictured below. After an undetermined number of years, the diner was enclosed with block walls. In the above photograph, note how the building's windows frame the bus windows. For most of its existence, the establishment was known as Dee's Diner, then briefly as Dolly's Diner. A very popular place to stop for breakfast or lunch, it stood on Foothill Boulevard, west of the Richfield service station and the Café Italiano. It was torn down in the early 1990s. (Both, Ed Dietl.)

The Kapu Kai restaurant, coffee shop, and bowling alley was certainly one of the most unusual places in Cucamonga's history. The large Polynesian-themed building stood on the northwest corner of Foothill Boulevard and Vineyard Avenue in the 1960s. Inside, there were several different dining rooms, ranging in style from casual to formal. Patrons could sit in thatched huts or have drinks in a Tahitian fire lounge. All of the decor was specially made, from the shell lamps to the giant tikis. On some nights, a lady with a large snake wrapped around her visited guests at their tables. (Both, Oceanic Arts.)

The Kapu Kai's coffee shop adjoined the bowling alley and provided a picturesque place for families and young people to gather. Sadly, the Kapu Kai was damaged beyond repair in the 1969 flood. Afterward, a roller rink operated on the site for a number of years. (Both, Oceanic Arts.)

5-COURSE DINNER $2.00

Soup   Lucy's Famous Salad   Antipasto

Spaghetti and Ravioli

Chicken or Steak

Dessert

Coffee, Tea, Milk or Buttermilk

No Half Portions Served

EXTRAS—Short Orders

Radishes and Celery............................25

French Fries 15

Lucy and John's began as a tiny coffee shop in the Cucamonga Market building before moving down the road to 8189 Foothill Boulevard, near the Sycamore Inn. Lucy and John's offered a five-course dinner for $2. Note the beverage choices. There were no bottomless glasses of soda or iced tea in 1947. But French fries could be had for 15¢! (Jane Vath O'Connell.)

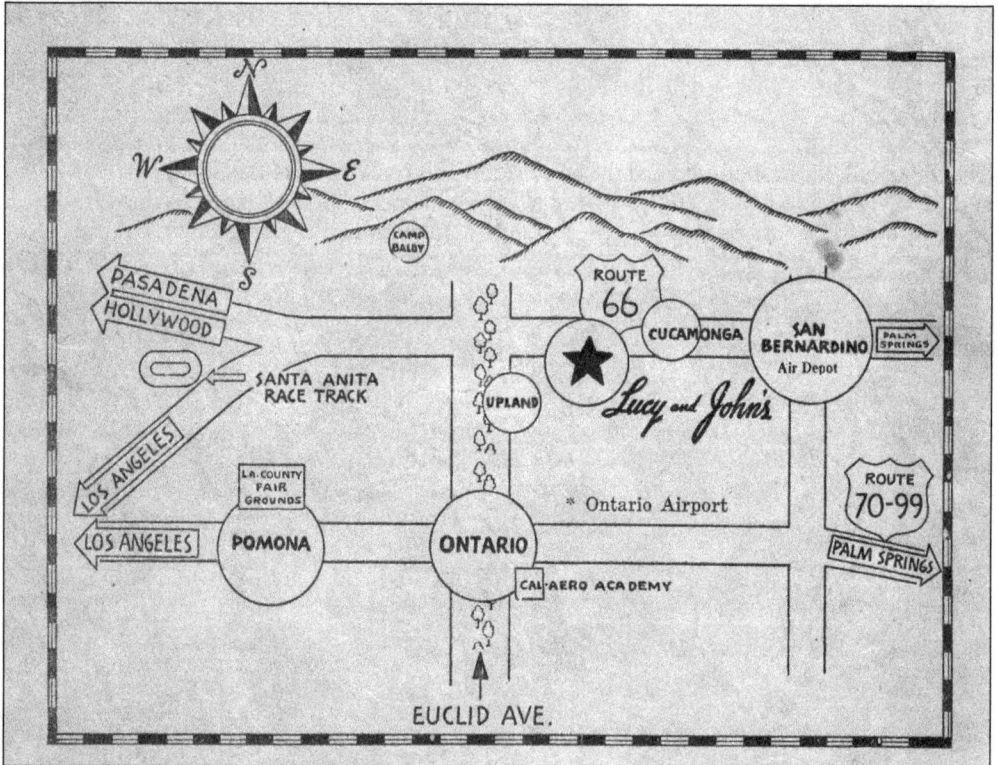

A widely out-of-scale map shows great Southland places to visit, presumably before or after having a meal at Lucy and John's restaurant. Notice the absence of today's freeway numbers. Routes 66, 70, and 99 (now Interstate 10) were highways with stop signs and traffic signals. (Jane Vath O'Connell.)

Shown above is Lucy and John's restaurant with its clean, modern design. Below is the same building after the new owners redesigned it. The story goes that the owners asked the staff for their ideas about a new theme for the restaurant. The winning suggestion was Aladdin and his magic lamp, hence the new name, Magic Lamp Inn. An Aladdin-styled lamp burns brightly at night along the road. The building's exterior received an elaborate makeover of layer tile and brickwork and opened in 1955. On careful inspection, the original plain white walls can be seen on the second story. (Above, Jane Vath O'Connell; below, Claude Ellena.)

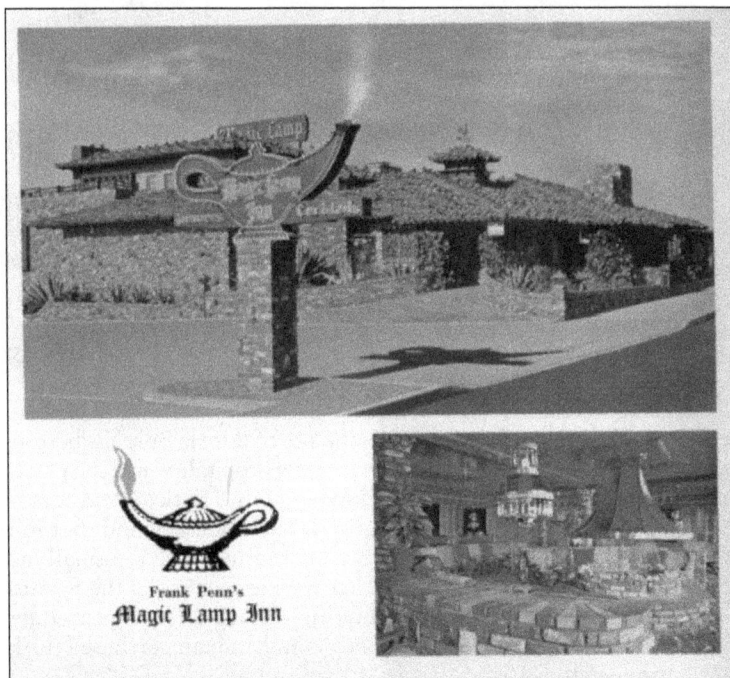

Frank Penn's
Magic Lamp Inn

The Sycamore Inn is a place of much history. It is the site of "Uncle Billy" Rubottom's Butterfield stage stop, the Mountain View Inn, known for its friendly hospitality. It is the place where Uncle Billy saved Doña Merced's life from a posse seeking vigilante justice. And it is where Ramon Carrillo, a relative of Doña Merced's second husband, was ambushed and shot in the back and died while escorting her carriage. Outside the Sycamore Inn, there is a small monument of a bear, erected by the Native Daughters of the Golden West in memory of the Spanish padres who camped here on their way to Monterey. Encountering a group of bears peacefully eating, they named the place Bear Gulch. In 1912, German-born John Klusman purchased the land and built the Bavarian-style inn seen today.

It was common practice for businesses to place holiday greetings advertisements in the *Cucamonga Times*. The location's history and Billy Rubottom's colorful life were added to the inn's décor around 1950, as seen in this holiday ad boasting a new "Billy Room" decorated in Old West style

59

The Kings of the Road Museum displayed classic and celebrity-owned automobiles. The museum was opened in 1954 by three automotive enthusiasts—Dr. Orris Myers, Purcell Ingram, and Orville Race. The name of the museum was taken from the title of the well-known Ken Purdy book that celebrated the evolution of the automobile. But the museum did not receive enough visitor traffic and closed in less than 20 years. (Jane Vath O'Connell.)

Numerous motels have come and gone along the old Route 66, but a few remain. The New Kansan, at the corner of Hellman Avenue and Foothill Boulevard, still operates as a motel and looks much the same as it did over 50 years ago.

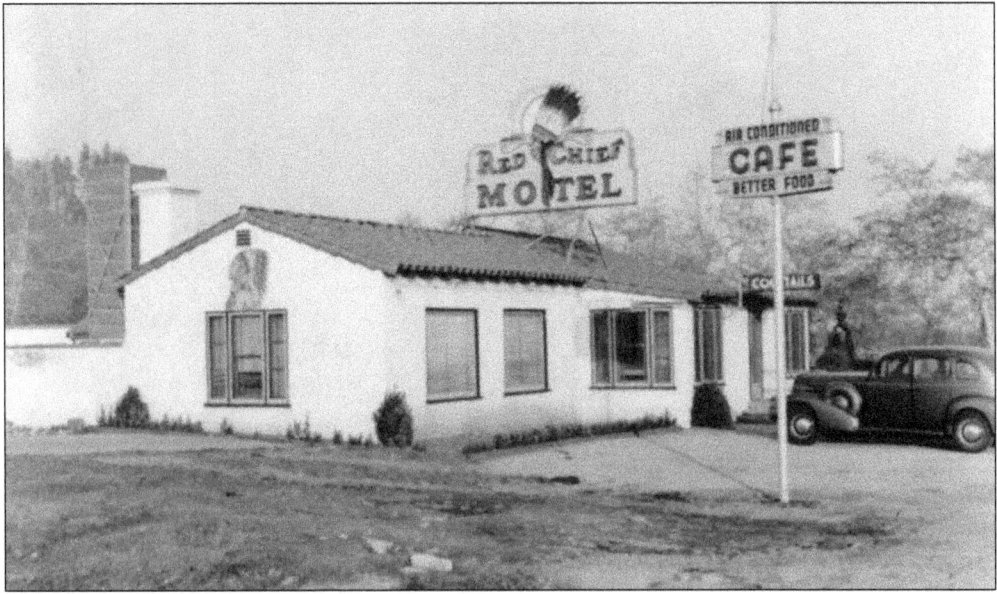

The Red Chief Motel, 8270 Foothill Boulevard, was located east of Sycamore Inn. Today, all that remains is the motel office building, which is now a restaurant. Like many motor courts, it was a group of small cottage-like bungalows. Traveling cross-country on mid-20th-century highways took longer than it does on today's high-speed freeways. Small themed motels such as this were common. (Both, Jane Vath O'Connell.)

William Harvey's Cucamonga Garage opened in 1914. The business is seen here in the 1920s as the Hugh Larson Ford Repair Shop, on the northwest corner of Archibald Avenue and Foothill Boulevard. The domed cylinders in front of the building are gas pumps. When the pump ran low, the station attendant would bring out a bucket of gasoline and pour it into the top of the pump. (Brancacio-Owen family.)

OVER 52 MILES
OF 1959 CARS

The quaint San Bernardino County countryside has an endless stream of new 1959 cars in a local advertisement for Bank of America. Known as Highway 66, Route 66, and, locally, as Foothill Boulevard, the Mother Road began in Chicago and ended at the Pacific Ocean. The route went straight through Cucamonga, bringing customers to gas stations, motels, and eateries. It lost its designation as a US highway in 1985.

Harvey added a Richfield gas station in front of his garage. It opened in 1927 as the Cucamonga Service Station (above c. 1927, below c. 1935). By 1940, Harvey had sold it to Woodrow and Morris. The mechanic's garage was owned by Virgil Davis, who also owned the Santa Fe service station in Northtown. The station's Mission Revival architecture, including arched entryways, made it a roadside beauty. The gas station operated until 1972. For decades, the structure stood vacant. The abandoned mechanic's garage collapsed in a rainstorm in 2011. In 2014, restoration of the station by local volunteers began, with the intent for it to become a Route 66 visitor center and museum. (Both, Shirley O'Morrow and Ed Dietl.)

When the men went off to war, women had to take over some of the traditional male duties, such as car maintenance. Faye Perdew, in 1943, fixed her own car while her husband was serving in World War II. Money was tight for her. She was already soldering airplane controls for the war effort. Perdew figured that if she could do that, she could change the oil in the car. And she did. (Perdew and Carpena families.)

An unidentified young man fills up the tank at the Cucamonga Service Station around 1940. Gas stations, also known as service stations, offered a lot of free services. When a car pulled up to the pumps, not only did the attendant fill the gas tank, but he cleaned the windows and checked the oil, water, and tire pressure as well. The term *self-service* would not appear at gas stations until the 1970s. (Ed Dietl.)

Three

NORTHTOWN

Nico (left), Ray "Vevito" (center), and Rachel Torres pose in their front yard in 1945. In those days, children were expected to entertain themselves outside while adults worked. The Torreses played marbles, rode bikes, and flew kites. Their parents, Ramon "Guerro" and Aurora "China" Torres, like many Northtown residents, labored at Guasti's Italian Vineyard Company. Northtown got its name from its position relative to Guasti, which used to be called South Cucamonga. When Secondo Guasti built his enormous vineyard and winery, many laborers lived in the little town *north* of it, called North Cucamonga. Today, this neighborhood in southern Rancho Cucamonga is called Northtown. The map on page 21 illustrates how "north" is south and how "south" was actually north. (Northtown Community Center.)

The Trancosa family came to Northtown in 1901. Arnulfo Trancosa holds baby Nettie Trancosa in 1906. The man at left is not identified. The early 20th century was a busy time in Cucamonga. Many immigrants were coming to the United States and to Cucamonga, most seeking work. The thousands of acres of vineyards and orchards, as well as the wineries and related businesses, provided jobs for these immigrants. (Northtown Community Center.)

Large ranches in and near Northtown, such as those owned by Milliken, Lucas, and Hofer, employed many residents. Smaller family farms hired seasonal laborers from Northtown as well. The Stipe family arrived from Arkansas in 1917. They owned a peach orchard and the first dairy in Northtown. Will and Maggie Stipe pose here in 1909 with three of their children. Shown are, from left to right, Homer, Will, Tressie, Maggie, and Bessie. (Lucille Thompson.)

The border-crossing fee was only one penny when Irineo Jimenez (pictured) brought his wife and family and all their belongings to California in 1909. Their long journey began when Jimenez heroically rescued their daughter and 10-month-old grandbaby from an abusive marriage in Mexico. Jimenez settled his family in Northtown and opened a small market. As money was saved, he and his wife bought other property in the neighborhood. Much of that property was sold when he fell ill and his daughter needed to pay medical bills for her dying father. Jimenez's descendants remain in Northtown. His great-granddaughter works to provide housing and programs for area residents. (Northtown Community Center.)

Built in 1887, the Santa Fe train depot at Eighth Street and Archibald Avenue served the many fruit growers and other businesses in Cucamonga and Ioamosa (Alta Loma). Nearby were many packinghouses that loaded their freight onto trains bound for cities in the East. When the first train depot burned down, a simple Art Deco station was built as its replacement. In addition to shipping grapes, peaches, and citrus, the trains carried residents to shop or attend business in Ontario or Los Angeles. (City of Rancho Cucamonga.)

This Cucamonga packinghouse was located on Eighth Street, east of Archibald Avenue. Grapes, citrus, and fresh and canned fruit were shipped to market from here. The train depot is seen on the right.

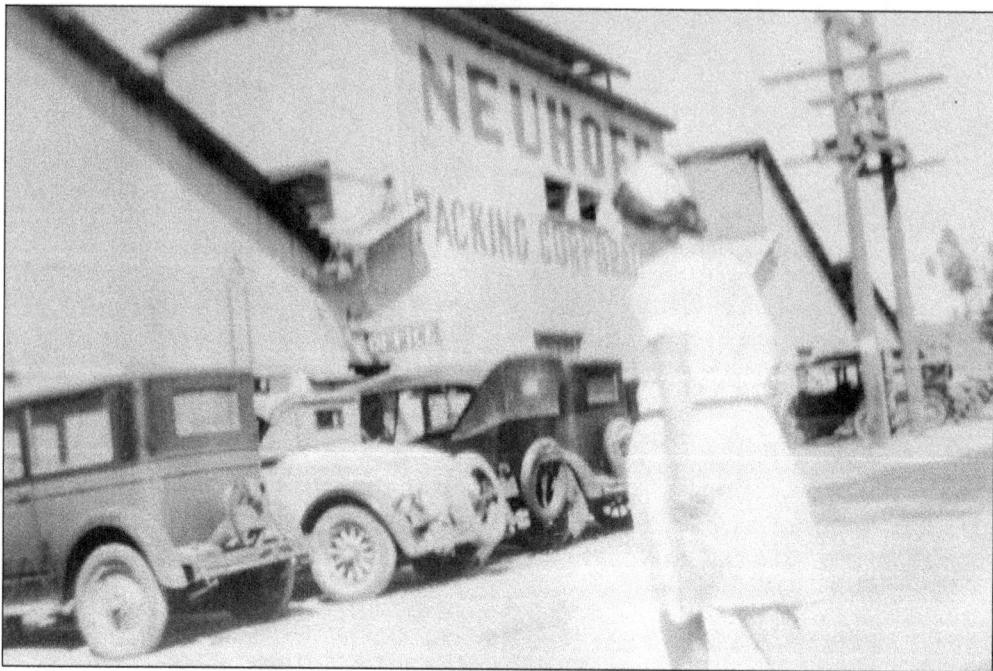

Lena Davis walks toward the cannery to go to work north of the tracks on Eighth Street. Women in the cannery wore a white or green uniform and hat in the cannery. The citrus packinghouse, where the women would wrap oranges individually in paper, did not require such attire. When the Neuhoff cannery closed, peaches were trucked to Hemet for canning. (Lucille Thompson.)

Santa Fe Railway workers ride *La Carrochita*, the little carriage, in the 1940s. Foreman Luis Sanchez, in front on the right side of the handle, and his workers repaired the tracks and replace railroad ties. Some railroad laborers such as these were braceros, legal temporary workers from Mexico. They took up various labor jobs in addition to the usual fieldwork. (Northtown Community Center.)

Known simply as Maco's Barbershop by the locals, this establishment was located at Center and Humboldt Avenues. Here, Maco Rodriguez gives a young customer a trim in the late 1960s. (Northtown Community Center.)

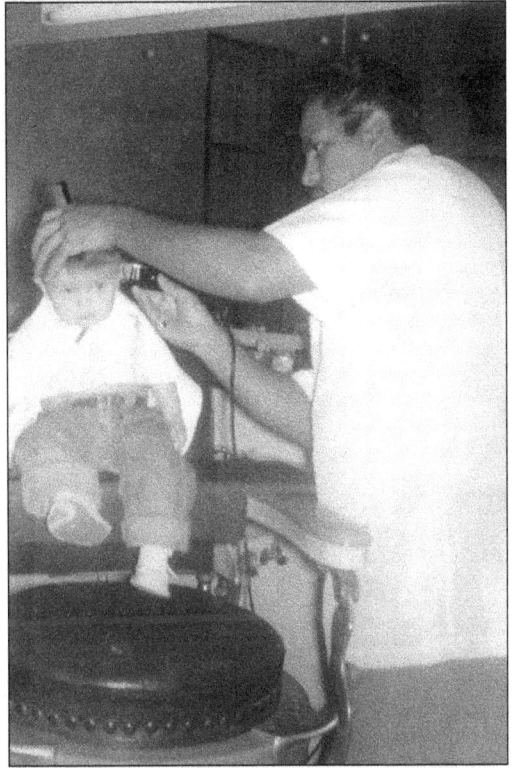

Santolucitos butcher shop was famous for the delicious meats sold there. Residents still remember the tantalizing smells of the Italian spices and sausages. It was first located on Arrow Highway and Hermosa Avenue. Pictured here are Guido (left) and Bob. After the Santolucitos family closed the shop, Guido continued the business under his own name as an Italian deli. He sold the deli in 2015.

Our Lady of Mount Carmel Church still stands at the corner of Hermosa Avenue and Eighth Street, a few steps from the old Padre Winery. Here, Father Valdez presides among the ornate décor, including the Virgin Mary, placed on the walls. A center of the Northtown community for many families, the Catholic church was where babies were baptized and children received their First Communions, and where people were married and the dead were honored. (Northtown Community Center.)

Ramon Rodriguez and his new bride, Lupe, pose for wedding photographs at Our Lady of Mount Carmel Church around 1939. One day, their son Maco would own a barbershop in Northtown. Even on one of the happiest days of a person's life, there was no smiling for the camera then. Formal photographs dictated somber expressions, no matter the occasion. (Northtown Community Center.)

Grieving Northtown families somberly proceed out of the Our Lady of Mount Carmel with their deceased loved one around 1940. Possibly, there had been a wake the night before in the old Franklin schoolhouse, as most homes did not have enough room for a crowd. Cucamonga had no cemetery. Most families used Bellevue Cemetery in Ontario or one of the cemeteries in Pomona as a place to bury their dead. (Northtown Community Center.)

Ernestina Carpena and Rufus Putnam "Doc" Perdew were married at Our Lady of Mount Carmel Church on January 20, 1922. Both were from pioneer families. Doc's parents had come to California in 1861 and settled in Grapeland, now Etiwanda. Ernestina's father, Frank Cardena, emigrated from Mexico in 1870. Cardena was a vineyardist with a farm at Turner Avenue and Eighth Street. They had two children, Faye and Donald. Doc worked as a laborer and Ernestina as a citrus packer. (Perdew and Carpena families.)

The Franklin District Schoolhouse opened in 1892 on Twenty-Fourth Street to serve the North Cucamonga children. Like many rural schools, it opened with one teacher instructing all the grades. About 1908, a second teacher was added. When the new Cucamonga School was built on Archibald Avenue in 1916, the Franklin School was no longer needed, and it was closed shortly after. Franklin's school bell was transferred to the new school. (Lucille Thompson.)

The Cucamonga School District began inside the Rains House in 1870. The second Cucamonga School was on San Bernardino Road. By 1916, another school was needed. To serve children in the Northtown area, the Cucamonga School was built on Archibald Avenue, south of Eighth Street. Its Mission-style building was topped with a brass school bell, which was rung each morning to call the children to class. (Cucamonga School District.)

74

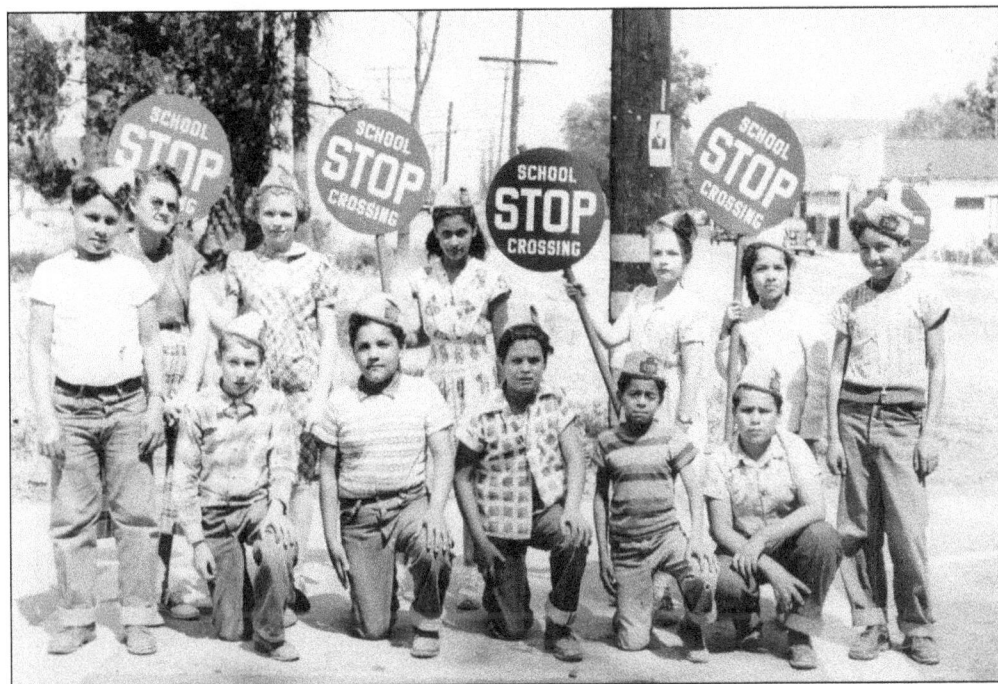

These Cucamonga School Safety Patrol students remind drivers to stop for children on busy Archibald Avenue in front of the school. It was common for children to walk a couple of miles to and from school along dirt roads and over train tracks. Former students remembered a principal who drove the large school car on rainy days to pick up students and bring them to school. (Cucamonga School District.)

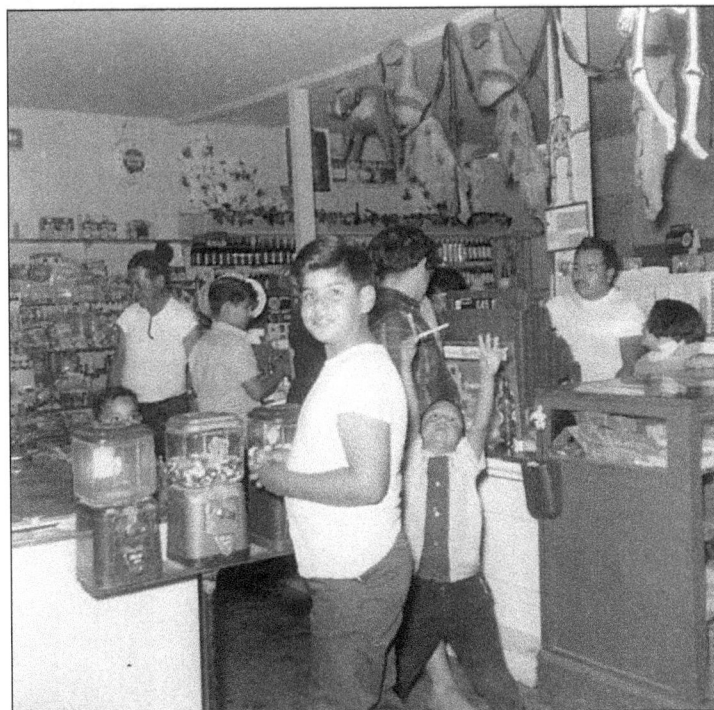

Kids select candy and treats and decide which piñata they would like for their birthday party in a local Northtown market. (Northtown Community Center.)

The Santa Fe gas station on Archibald Avenue and Eighth Street in Northtown was owned by Virgil Davis. A mechanic, he attended to the needs of residents' bicycles and automobiles. There was also a blacksmith shop on the premises, as horses were still used and farm equipment needed repair. Pictured here are Virgil's family members. Virgil's brother Isaac is at center. Virgil's wife, Lena, stands at right with their daughters Wanda and Adelle.

Pony pictures were an extremely popular Northtown item over the decades. A local photographer would walk down the street with a pony in tow. Word would spread, and, soon, mothers had toddlers dressed and ready to take a photograph. Faye Perdew, age two, poses happily in 1925 on Eighth Street. (Perdew and Carpena families.)

These Northtown children look like they have had a good day playing outside their home on Center Avenue. Fun could be had without fancy toys or electronics. Group games such as hide-and-seek and tag kept siblings and cousins busy for hours. Shown here are, from left to right, Lydia Rodriguez, Joe Rodriguez (standing), Leo Ramirez, Louie Rodriguez, and Ramon Rodriguez. (Northtown Community Center.)

Mary Olagues, age 16, takes a moment from her duties as a new mother in front of her home on Twenty-Sixth Street in 1952. An extraordinary thing about Northtown is the large number of families that have remained in the same neighborhood for generations. Cucamonga has grown from a town of just a few thousand residents in the early 1900s to a city with almost 200,000 in 2015. (Northtown Community Center.)

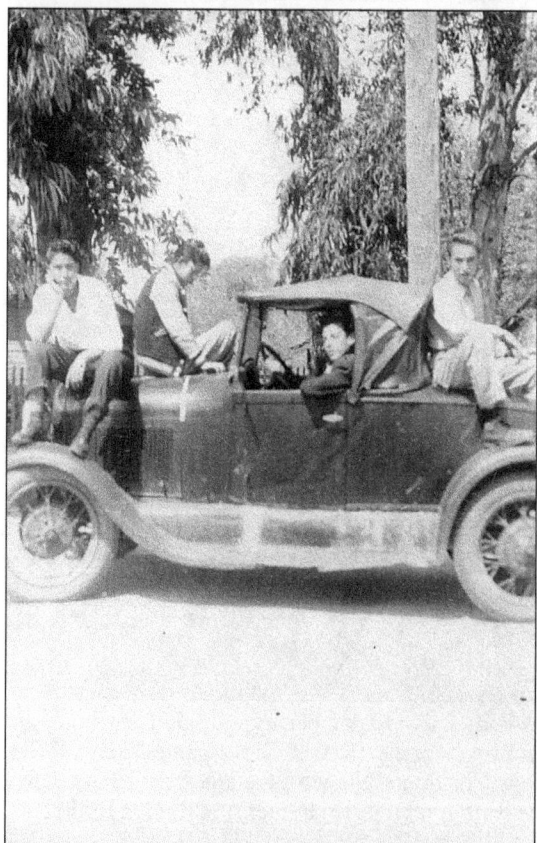

Learning to drive, a young man's rite of passage, is celebrated, no matter how old the car may be. Seen here are, from left to right, Jimmy Ramirez, Rudy Gonzales, Ramon Calavera, and Billy Norris. The boys try to look as cool and as suave as possible on a borrowed set of wheels. Automobiles brought freedom to travel and meet people and to find work and entertainment away from home. (Northtown Community Center.)

Since the first car rolled off an assembly line, people have loved posing with their new sets of wheels. Bessie Stipe stands in front of the Cucamonga Fruit Association packinghouse with her father's 1929 Ford. She regularly drove her father, who had poor eyesight. (Lucille Thompson.)

Virgil Davis had dreams of racing in a new contest called the Indianapolis 500, which had begun in 1911. Being a handy mechanic, he built his No. 9 race car from the wheels up from parts he could find or make, whenever he was not fixing other people's cars in his Santa Fe Garage. He drove No. 9 in local races. Sadly, he never got to the big one in Indiana. (Shirley O'Morrow.)

The Franklin Schoolhouse building continued to be used for another 40 years. First, it was a picture house for "flickers" (silent movies). Next, it was a dance hall. The Church of the Nazarene then occupied it for several years. After that, it was a pool hall, a beer tavern, and, lastly, the Montezuma Café, until it could no longer meet building standards in 1954. (Northtown Community Center.)

One day in the 1920s, a brief surprise arrived at the Santa Fe train station. A very tall man stepped out onto the platform to stretch his legs. He told curious onlookers he was the world's tallest man. He graciously stood for a photograph, then boarded the train again. Where he was from or where he was going, no one remembers. All that remains is this photograph. (Lucille Thompson.)

Four

WORKING THE LAND

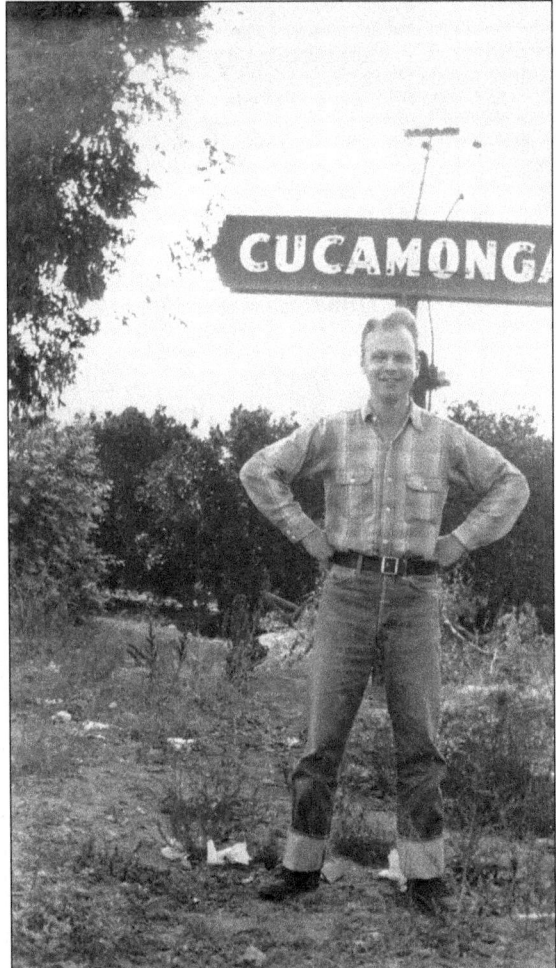

According to the back of this photograph, this unidentified young man stopped on his way to Lake Arrowhead in 1948 to pose in front of a Cucamonga orange grove. Quite possibly, it was snapped to send to envious relatives in the snowy East. Or, perhaps it was to prove there really was a Cucamonga, as folks had heard on Jack Benny's radio show. Celebrities, including Benny, and even regular folk stopped at Cucamonga wineries on their way to places like Palm Springs and Lake Arrowhead. Until the late 1970s, the area was quite rural, with family-run orchards and wineries throughout Cucamonga, Alta Loma, and Etiwanda. Many families owned an orchard in addition to their primary business. (Jane Vath O'Connell.)

This advertisement from the late 1800s would have been sent to cities near and far. Residents would also send advertisements like these in letters to their friends and families in other states to encourage them to move to Cucamonga. After the foreclosure of John Rains's Cucamonga Rancho, property dealers like Isaias Hellman created real estate companies, such as the Cucamonga Fruit Lands Company and the Cucamonga Homestead Company, to buy and sell the acreage. The weather, available water, and proximity to the railroad were key concerns for a farmer. Would the crops grow? Could the fruit be shipped quickly before it spoiled? These announcements promised it all and brought many new ranchers to the Cucamonga area. (Ontario Library.)

The Wattenburger family came to Cucamonga in the early 1900s. Here, family members proudly pose at their home on Archibald Avenue in front of their heavily laden orange trees that are ready for harvest. Notice some of the playful poses with oranges in an otherwise somber photograph. (Jackie Cartwright Jeffers.)

Young Gene Billings, the future Alta Loma fire chief, and his grandfather look ready to plow the weeds between the orange trees near their house on Archibald Avenue. Horses were an important part of the farm until the advent of the tractor. A few years after this photograph was taken, the Billings family moved to Alta Loma and opened the Billings Market on Amethyst Avenue. (Billings family.)

GOLD MEDAL WINNING

Fresh Rich Milk

From Cucamonga's Only
100% LOCAL DAIRY

Allura Farm Dairy

8809 GROVE
Call Yu. 2-3653
For Home Delivery

Home milk delivery was quite common, as this c. 1960 advertisement from the *Cucamonga Times* indicates. The milkman, often dressed in white, drove his truck from house to house in the early hours of the morning. Glass bottles of milk clinked in their wire basket as he set down the customer's regular order by the door. He would take away the basket of empty milk bottles the home owner had left on the porch the night before. Sometimes, there would be a note asking for an extra item, such as a pint of cream or buttermilk. The delivery man would fetch that from his truck and put it on the porch before driving to the next house. The Allura Farm Dairy still exists today on Grove Avenue, but only as a drive-through dairy with new owners and no cows.

This aerial photograph of the Christmas House at the northwest corner of Archibald and Sixth Avenues in the mid-1900s shows that it was once surrounded by citrus groves, with a large chicken ranch behind it on the west side. Chicken or egg ranches were another common type of farm in Cucamonga. (Ed Dietl.)

The Stipe farm on Turner Avenue by Northtown had a dairy from 1917 to 1922. Lucille Stipe is checking on the family's cows and hay barn with her father, William Stipe. Large grocery chains so common today were not widespread yet. Local farmers were depended upon to supply the community with much of its food. (Lucille Thompson.)

Prior to 2000, newcomers to Rancho Cucamonga were often surprised to find flocks of sheep around town, such as these on Arrow Highway. For decades, Basque shepherds on horseback, accompanied by their sheepdogs, grazed their flocks in Cucamonga's many open fields. Eventually, the vacant land was built upon, and the sheep and their herders had to move elsewhere for greener pastures. (Sheryl Muskatell.)

In 1939, peach farmer William Stipe holds baby Lucille as his laborers get ready to harvest 120 acres of peaches. Peach harvest always began on August 20. A week before, Stipe would go into Northtown and announce that whoever wanted work could show up on the August 20 to pick peaches. Workers climbed tall ladders to gently pick the fruit. The Stipes sent their peaches to a cannery in Hemet, where they were sorted and graded. If any peaches were not the right size, the whole load was sent back. Some of the crop was sold fresh, as table fruit. A great deal of it was sent to the cannery. Canneries in Ontario, Cucamonga, Pomona, Kingsburg, and Van Nuys joined to form Golden State Canneries. The venture ran into financial problems and dissolved eight years later. Hemet Packing Co. officially took over on January 8, 1924. (Above, Lucille Thompson.)

VILLA

SELECTED CALIFORNIA FRUIT PACKED BY GOLDEN STATE CANNING CO ONTARIO & CUCAMONGA CAL.

SELECTED CALIFORNIA FRUIT PACKED BY GOLDEN STATE CANNING CO ONTARIO & CUCAMONGA CAL.

NET CONTENTS 6 LBS. 4 OZ.

PACKED WITHOUT SUGAR, SWEETEN TO TASTE.

YELLOW FREE PEACHES

During the Depression, William Stipe happened to remove his aged peach trees. The government recommended that farmers leave some fields fallow, compensating the owners and giving them soil conditioners to plow into the earth to avoid another Dust Bowl. Stipe did not want a field of weeds. Instead, he planted potatoes to help people. Potatoes were a cheap food people could buy during those lean years. Stipe planted peaches again a few years later. (Lucille Thompson.)

One of the Thomas brothers harvests corn around 1930. Sometimes, additional crops for family use were grown, in addition to the cash crop. Or, different crops were rotated in to give the soil a chance to regain nutrients. Corn demands a great deal of water in the soil to fully develop. It is unusual to see this crop in Cucamonga. (Ontario Library.)

In 1911, Shotaro Yamaguchi emigrated from Japan in search of land to start a fruit ranch. He went first to Mexico, but then heard about Cucamonga. Yamaguchi purchased a 10-acre strip of land along present-day Church Street between Hellman and Carnelian Avenues and then set out avocado saplings. He built a house and barn, and even a Japanese bathhouse for personal use in the backyard. Once his farm was established, Yamaguchi traveled home to Japan in 1923 to find a bride. The following year, he returned with his new wife, Yosheia. During World War II, the Yamaguchis and their children and five grandchildren were interned in a camp in Arizona. Fortunately, their foreman, Jesus Mendoza of Northtown, cared for the farm in their absence, and the Yamaguchis had a home and livelihood to return to. (Bill Yamaguchi.)

Bill Yamaguchi is dwarfed by the giant grapefruit and hybrids his grandfather Shotaro Yamaguchi grew in his garden. As a hobby, Shotaro experimented in creating hybrids. Sometimes, a tree bearing several types of fruit was created. Other trees produced crossbred fruit. (Bill Yamaguchi.)

Who can resist taking a photograph contrasting sunny California lemons with winter's snowy mountains? Most Cucamonga scrapbooks have at least one of these picturesque shots of Cucamonga Peak. The dirt path running horizontally across the photograph would one day be Church Street. Walking east, or right, would lead one to the stone Methodist church on Archibald Avenue. (Bill Yamaguchi.)

It took a team of six horses and mules to pull the tank of spray that protected the citrus trees from fungus and insects. On top on the wagon are some of the men of the Stipe family. William Stipe grew oranges on Ninth Street in addition to his peaches. Farmers had to know the specific type of care each crop or animal needed. (Lucille Thompson.)

There are reminders of its history everywhere in Cucamonga. This grape-crusher building and lemon trees near Hermosa Avenue and Baseline Road were once part of the Sanchez Winery. Old barns sagging in backyards, rusty smudge pots used as mailbox stands, vacant lots with abandoned grapevines, and rows of lemon trees by a house are reminders of Cucamonga's agricultural roots. (Jane Vath O'Connell.)

HEADQUARTERS FOR ALL BUILDING REQUIREMENTS

Lumber and Supplies

ALSO A COMPLETE FEED LINE

You need not search farther for a complete and satisfactory line of high quality feeds. We have a large list of satisfied users in the Cucamonga community and know you too will be one if you give us a trial. Stop in and visit over your building and feed problems.

Joe Vizio   Ben J. Vizio

CUCAMONGA LUMBER YARD & FEED STORE

8744 Archibald Ave., Cucamonga . . . YU. 2-1678

Lumberyards and feed stores have almost completely disappeared in Cucamonga. This advertisement dates to the late 1950s, when the town was still quite rural and service with a smile was still important. But the population was growing. Agriculture was beginning to move out. Fewer and fewer residents needed to feed horses and chickens. Tract homes came ready-made. The giant home centers took the place of neighborhood lumberyards and feed stores.

91

The majestic Cucamonga Valley was said to be reminiscent of Italy's Piedmont region, at the foot of the snowcapped Alps. The temperate winters and hot summers create sweet grapes just right for wine-making or for the table. The roots of grapevines can extend down through the sandy soil nearly 20 feet to reach water. The ability to grow a crop without irrigation brought many ranchers and vintners to the Cucamonga Valley. (Ontario Library.)

Harold B. Anderson Sr. inspects a vineyard on Dog Ridge for disease about 1950. He was the county agricultural inspector, working out of an office on Archibald Avenue, north of Foothill Boulevard. Insects and diseases can quickly wipe out a crop. Anaheim disease, now called Pierce's disease, and phylloxera wiped out vineyards in the Los Angeles basin. That region then turned from grapes to citrus crops. The warm, dry air of the Cucamonga Valley and its deep, sandy soils seemed to protect the vineyards from Pierce's disease. But then a new problem arrived—a man-made one: smog. The change in air quality in the 1960s and 1970s turned grape leaves yellow, affecting the growth of the fruit. That added to changes in property values, and much of the wine-making left the Cucamonga Valley. (Karen Stanfield.)

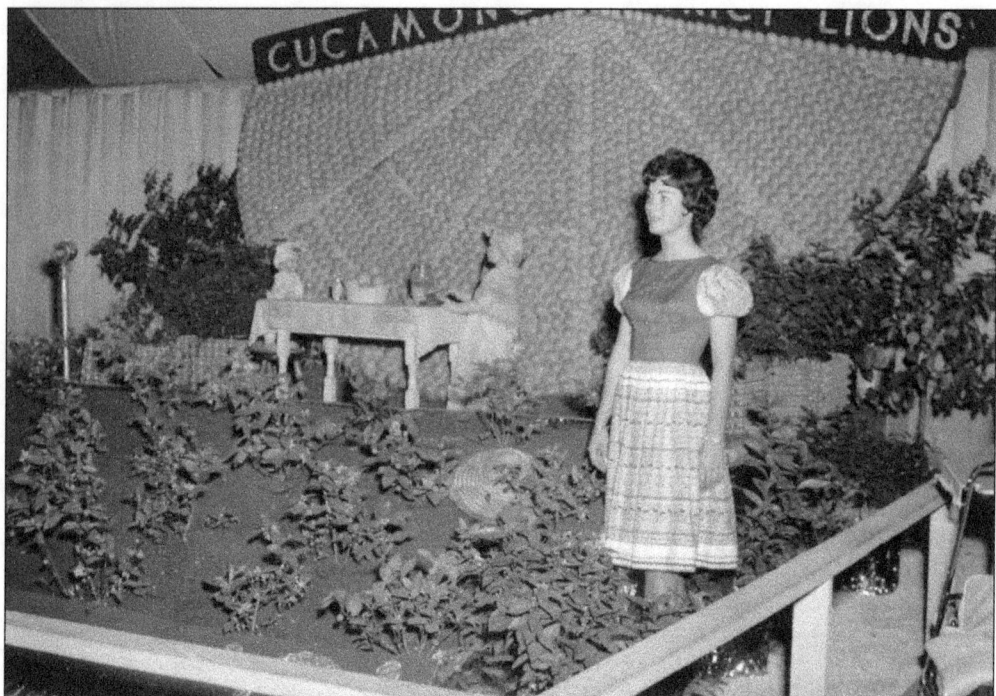

Emily Blatnick, age 19, was Miss Cucamonga 1962 when she represented the Cucamonga chapter of the Lions Club at the San Bernardino Orange Show. Prizes were awarded to the best displays. (Mary Blatnick.)

CUCAMONGA BELLE
CUCAMONGA FOOTHILL ORANGE ASSN.

Much like the labels on canned goods, the fruit-crate label served the dual purpose of identification and advertising. The colorful and often fanciful paper labels glued to the ends of the wooden crates as brand identifiers have become sought-after artwork.

Five

WINERIES

The Cucamonga Wine district had over 50 wineries, ranging from small family businesses, such as the Thomas Winery, to large companies run by Garrett and the Vai brothers. Until World War II, Cucamonga was the source of most American wine. Dark, heavier table wines, such as burgundy, led market sales. Soldiers serving in Europe in the early 1940s were introduced to a variety of lighter wines. Those veterans came home wanting to buy those flavors of wine to share at home. New vintners started planting in the Napa region of Northern California and began making lighter wines. Meanwhile, property taxes became a huge problem for all types of ranchers in the Cucamonga area. It was too expensive for many to keep their property. Land developers bought the acreages, and urban sprawl took over the vineyards and orchards. (Marsha Banks.)

D'ye Like Wine?

——If so, let your judgment
set the standard in wines.

——Your answer is

OLD RANCHO BRAND

——at California's Oldest Winery—now in
its 104th year — established nearly
44 years before the Model Colony
was settled.

•

CUCAMONGA VINTAGE COMPANY

N. E. Corner of Foothill Blvd.
and Vineyard Ave.

Cucamonga - • - California

A 1942 advertisement promotes Old Rancho Brand wine from the Cucamonga Vintage Company, now remembered as the Thomas Winery. Writers employed by the WPA in the 1930s determined that the Thomas Vineyards winery was the oldest in the state of California. The Old Rancho Wines brand gives a nod to the winery's beginnings on Tapia's Cucamonga Rancho in 1838. John Rains purchased the Cucamonga Rancho from Tapia's heirs in 1858 and expanded the vineyard by planting 125,000 vines. After Rains's death and the rancho's foreclosure, Isaias Hellman and his business partners owned the property from 1873 to 1917. Captain Garcia, Motsinger, and J.L. Sansevain were some of the property managers/investors during that time. (City of Rancho Cucamonga.)

In 1920, Hugh and Ida Thomas purchased the winery plus 450 acres of vineyards from the estate of George D. Haven. Hugh Thomas, an immigrant, was a native of Cardiff, Wales. Like Haven, Thomas had made his wealth in mining before turning to ranching. The Thomas Winery is seen here in 1968, after the Filippi family purchased it from the Thomas estate. (Cooper Museum.)

After a brief illness in 1938, Hugh Thomas died, leaving his finances in a precarious state. With the help of his brother, Richard Thomas, his sons were able to revive and continue the winery's business until the death of son Webster in 1965. The Filippi family owned the winery from 1967 to the mid-1980s, when it was sold to a property company. Here, Thomas's sons Webster (left) and Clifford (right) enjoy a car show at the winery in 1954. An unidentified man stands in the center. (City of Rancho Cucamonga.)

After their father died, Webster and Clifford Thomas served in World War II. Webster (left) served as a Navy lieutenant commander, and Clifford was a pilot. In the below photograph, Clifford (on the right) is seen in Egypt. Webster, widowed as a young man, fell in love with a Chinese woman in Hong Kong. He spent much of his time there, as her Chinese ties prevented her from entering the United States. In 1964, Webster died, leaving all his property to the Chinese woman. Unable to raise the cash needed to fulfill his brother's will, Clifford sold the beloved family winery in March 1967. By this time, both his mother, Ida, and an uncle, Richard, who helped run the business, had also passed away. One year later, Clifford, in poor health and grieving the sale of the historic winery, drove into a grove with a shotgun and ended his life.

This 1909 pastel drawing by R.C. Ford shows the small adobe building on the east side of the Thomas Winery. It is possibly the original winery Tapia built in the mid-1800s. As a boutique winery and tasting room, this part of the building continues the nearly 200-year tradition of wine-making.

From 1967 to the mid-1980s, the Filippi family owned and operated the winery. The main building now contains a restaurant and a coffeehouse. The grape-crushing building (left) is a retail shop. In the very early years, a waterwheel was used to power a grape crusher. In these tall buildings, grapes were lifted by conveyor belt into the top windows and fed into a motorized crusher below. (Ed Dietl.)

Italian immigrant Secondo Guasti founded the Italian Vineyard Company (IVC) in 1883 in South Cucamonga. He brought families from his native Italy and provided them with jobs, housing, a school, a firehouse, and a Catholic church. By 1917, IVC was the world's largest contiguous vineyard, with over 5,000 acres of vines. The Cucamonga-Guasti Regional Park bears his name, in honor of his great influence in Cucamonga's history. (Al Scorsatto.)

Vintners and grape growers meet in front of the beautiful stone buildings of the Italian Vineyard Company. During Prohibition, IVC merged with several other wineries and formed Fruit Industries, Ltd., which later became the California Wine Association. The combination of Guasti's son's death in 1932 and the effects of Prohibition were more than the winery could overcome. In 1945, IVC was purchased by Garrett & Company. In the 1950s, it was operated as Brookside Winery. (City of Rancho Cucamonga.)

A group of Guasti's coopers sits outside one of the winery's stone buildings in the early 1900s. Other winery companies have owned the land and buildings over the decades, but Guasti's name remains attached to that area, now part of the city of Ontario. The San Secondo d'Asti Catholic Church, north of Ontario International Airport, is the only Guasti building still in use. (City of Rancho Cucamonga.)

The world's largest vineyard had its own train system, connecting its vineyards and winery buildings. In the scorching summer sun, workers would load the sweet, heavy fruit into the railcars, which then transported the crop to the crusher building. The grapes were shoveled onto conveyers, which moved them into a crusher that squeezed out the juice that would be made into wine. (City of Rancho Cucamonga.)

In this photograph, Eighth Street runs east-west in front of the Padre Winery. On the left is Hermosa Avenue, with Our Lady of Mount Carmel Church occupying the corner. The tall white distillery building for making brandies stands at center, behind the main winery building. The original winery was founded in 1870. The Vai family purchased the winery in 1900. Champagne cellars, storage rooms, a great fermenting room, fortifying rooms, a laboratory, distillery, refrigeration system, machine shops, and a cooperage made up the modern winery, covering several acres. In addition to using the vast supply of grapes from its vineyards, the winery purchased a great amount from independent growers to keep up with demand for its products. (Al Scorsatto.)

Brothers Giovanni "John" (left) and Giacomo "Jim" represented the Vai family, who entered the wine business in 1900. The Vais were some of the original investors in the Italian Vineyard Company with Secondo Guasti and others, purchasing 1,200 acres in South Cucamonga. Guasti focused on building his Italian Vineyard Company. Meanwhile, the Vai family purchased a winery in North Cucamonga, which they renamed the Padre Winery, and began producing notable wine. (Cooper Museum.)

Padre wine is being dumped into the streets by federal law enforcement officials in a dramatic move during Prohibition near the company's main office on Alameda Street in Los Angeles. Prohibition was enacted in 1920 and lasted 13 years, ending in 1933. It banned the sale, production, importation, and transportation of alcoholic beverages. The production of sacramental wine was allowed in small amounts for churches, and households were permitted to make a limited amount of wine for home use. Some wineries turned to making wine vinegar to stay in business. Some packaged a juice to wine concentrate for markets. It had a "warning" that instructed buyers not to let the grape juice sit in a dark closet for a month or it would become wine. During Prohibition, the wineries changed their listing in the phone book to "fruit industries." When Prohibition ended, the Cucamonga Winery Company sent a cases of wine to Pres. Franklin Roosevelt on a Padre Winery truck. (Biane family.)

Giacomo Vai e l'automobile "reclame"

"Giacomo [Jim] Vai and the Advertising Car" is the translation for this advertisement, found in the 1928 book *Italians in California* by the Italian newspaper *L'Italo-Americano* of Los Angeles, California. During Prohibition, wineries had to get creative to stay in business. One product many wineries marketed was a medicinal elixir sold in drugstores. With a wink and a nod, these elixirs were promoted as health tonics that strengthened the blood and body. Oddly enough, these "medicinal" liquids sold in pharmacies often had a higher alcohol content than normal wine and spirits. The Vais' masterful use of advertising and marketing techniques, including using celebrities, was one of the reasons the company succeeded during and after Prohibition. (Al Scorsatto.)

Wine vats could hold upward of 60,000 gallons of product. Originally, oak barrels were brought around Cape Horn (South America) from Europe. Then, it was discovered that the tall redwood trees of Northern California made excellent wood for the coopers to construct barrels and vats. The vats shown here are in the Virginia Dare Winery. (City of Rancho Cucamonga.)

In 1909, the Vai family rebuilt the winery, adding the beautiful stonework arches that can be seen today on Eighth Street, just west of Hermosa Avenue. It was founded as the Padre Vineyard Company and later renamed the Cucamonga Vineyard Company, though it was always known as Padre Winery. Here, Padre tanker trucks are proudly displayed. During this time, it was considerably less expensive to ship alcohol in bulk than in individual bottles. Distributors across the country would bottle and label the wines to sell in area stores. At one time, the winery's yearly production included the following: 4.5 million gallons of fine wine and vermouths in huge, redwood storage vats; 7,000 barrels of brandy; and 500,000 bottles of champagne and sparkling wines. That averaged to 5,000 cases daily. (City of Rancho Cucamonga.)

The Biane family is one of the oldest continuing wine-making families in California. It began with the Vache family arriving in California in 1830 from Bordeaux, France. By 1883, they opened Brookside Winery in Redlands. Another young Frenchman, Marius Biane, arrived in 1892, fell in love, and married Marceline Vache. They continued wine-making in the Brookside Winery until Marius bought vineyards in Cucamonga. Brookside was then sold. In 1916, their sons Philo and François Biane went to work for Garrett & Company in Guasti. (City of Rancho Cucamonga.)

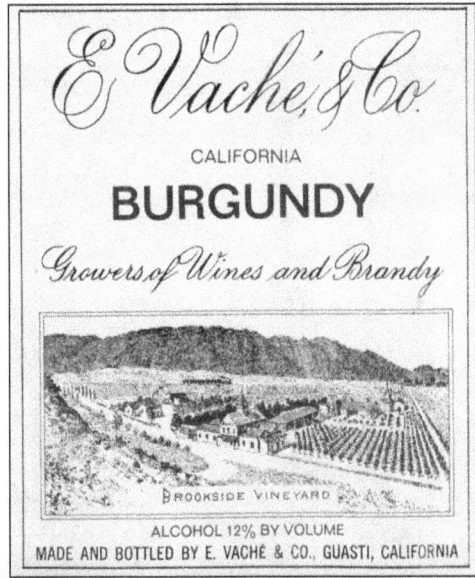

E. Vaché, & Co.

CALIFORNIA

BURGUNDY

Growers of Wines and Brandy

BROOKSIDE VINEYARD

ALCOHOL 12% BY VOLUME
MADE AND BOTTLED BY E. VACHÉ & CO., GUASTI, CALIFORNIA

Philo Biane (depicted in the painting) had two sons, Michael (left) and Pierre. In 1952, Philo reestablished Vache's Brookside Winery on the old Guasti property. Pierre purchased the Cucamonga Vineyard Company in 1976 and renamed it the Biane Winery. It produced vintages for a number of years, but is now inactive. The Biane family continues its nearly 200-year-old wine-making tradition on a small scale at Rancho de Philo in Alta Loma. (Ed Dietl.)

A special selection of wines has been chosen to make the cuvée for this award winning champagne

Primo F. Scorsatto

Champagne Master

CALIFORNIA BONDED WINERY NO. 1

SINCE 1870

Cucamonga Vineyard Co.

Cucamonga, California

California
BONDED WINERY No. 1

PRODUCED AND BOTTLED BY Cucamonga Vineyard Co.

Cucamonga, California • Alcohol 12% by Volume

FERMENTED IN THE BOTTLE

California

BRUT CHAMPAGNE

After Prohibition, every winery had to have a tax bond to operate legally. The Cucamonga Vineyard Company applied for and became the first in the United States to receive its bond. Though the number really did not signify anything other than that Cucamonga Vineyard was the first winery to send in its paperwork, the company boldly printed "Bonded Winery No. 1" on its labels as a marketing strategy. (Al Scorsatto.)

ALCOHOL 12% BY VOLUME   NET CONTENTS 4/5 QUART

Naturally Fermented

FOUR QUEENS HOTEL & CASINO

EXTRA DRY

California Champagne

Bulk Process-Sparkling Wine

DOWNTOWN • LAS VEGAS • NEVADA

PRODUCED AND BOTTLED BY Cucamonga Vineyard Co. CUCAMONGA, CALIFORNIA

Visiting glamorous Las Vegas meant drinking champagne at any one of the hotels and casinos. Each upscale hotel featured its own house champagne. What visitors did not know was that, whether it was the Aladdin, the Sahara, the Sands, or any other casino, all the house-brand champagnes came from the Padre Winery in Cucamonga, California. (Al Scorsatto.)

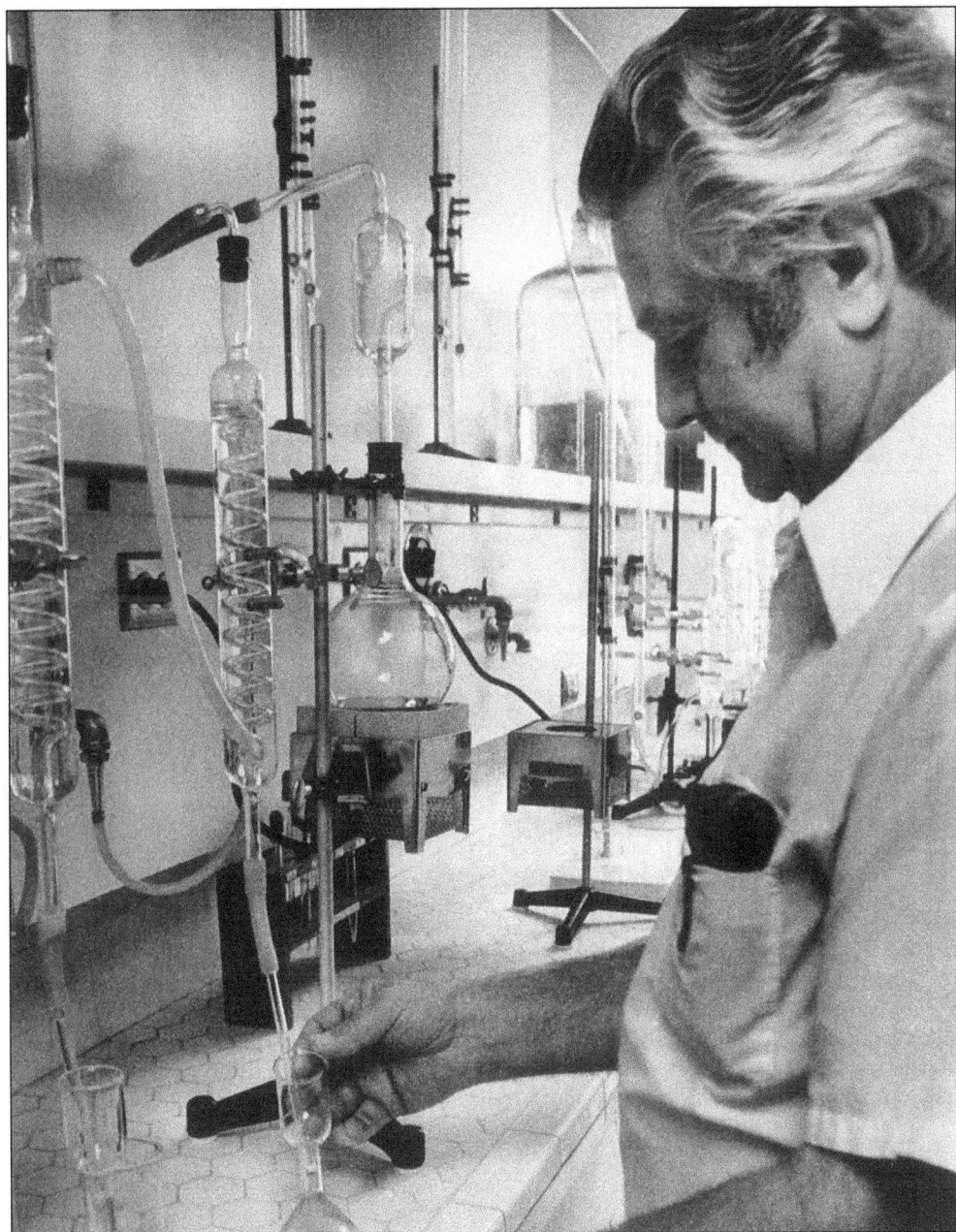

Primo Scorsatto perfected the champagne-maker's art for nearly 50 years at Padre. The secret to making award-winning wines and champagne is in the science. Here, he performs a titration test to determine the acid content of a wine in a fully equipped laboratory. So renowned were Scorsatto's skills that other wineries in the United States sent for him to help in correcting problems with their champagnes. On the way back from one such trip, a funny thing happened to Scorsatto. Seated in the plane's first-class section, he was offered a glass of champagne. He politely declined, having had enough through his day's work. The stewardess, unaware that the airline's champagne was a Padre vintage, and not knowing whom she was talking to, said he should try it, because it was quite good. Scorsatto good-naturedly smiled and said, "I know. I made it." (Al Scorsatto.)

In 1910, John Klusman purchased 1,000 acres of "wildland" in Cucamonga and planted a vineyard. He and his business partner, Morton Post, built the beautiful Mission Revival winery and named it the Mission Vineyard Company. In 1911, Garrett & Company from North Carolina purchased the Mission Winery, known today as the Virginia Dare. A few years later, Garrett & Company bought the famed Italian Vineyard Company in Guasti. After Garrett's death, the company sold its Cucamonga properties. The Virginia Dare had a series of owners until it was finally closed

and abandoned in 1961. On January 11, 1966, a fire destroyed the winery's roof and front office. During its years of abandonment, the property was periodically used for television shows requiring settings resembling bombed-out buildings in Europe, including *Combat!*, *The Rat Patrol*, and *The Invaders*. Many locals had fun watching the shows on television, searching the background of scenes for glimpses of modern cars driving by that did not belong in the shot. Today, the Virginia Dare serves as an office building at Haven Avenue and Foothill Boulevard. (Ontario Library.)

Seen here are Cucamonga Pioneer Winery employees preparing bottles for shipment and an aerial shot of the property that was located on South Haven Avenue. The winery was part of the Hofer Ranch whose lands spread across today's borders of Rancho Cucamonga and Ontario. The ranch began in 1882 as 10 acres purchased by Sanford Ballou sight unseen from Isaias Hellman. Ballou's son Bentley ran the ranch and increased it to 900 acres by 1915. After World War I, Bentley's nephew Paul Hofer arrived and became the ranch foreman. Hofer saved his money and gradually bought the ranchland from his uncle. In 1934, Hofer and Ballou organized the Cucamonga Pioneer Vineyard Association. The grape growers banded together to produce their own wine to have better control over the price of fruit and increase their profits. (Both, Ontario Library.)

ineries

Cucamonga Growers Co-Operative Winery E Calif blvd Ont	614-162
Cucamonga Pioneer Vineyard Assn S Haven av Cucmga	315-105
Cucamonga Valley Wine Co 1101 East A Ont	624-132
Cucamonga Vintage Co W Foothill blvd Cucmga	317-635
Cucamonga Wine Co 198 N Archibald av Cucmga	314-164
Cucamonga Winery S Rochester av Cucmga	315-131
Garrett & Co Inc 486 E Foothill blvd Cucmga	315-112
Italian Vineyard Co Guasti	612-133
Masi Bros Winery N Rochester av Cucmga	315-931
Padre Vineyard Co 429 E 8th Cucmga	311-15
Sanchez H Winery 550 N Turner av Cucmga	316-894

A page from the 1940 telephone directory shows many, but not all, of Cucamonga's wineries. The name "Cucamonga" was used often, since it carried a reputation for fine wine. Numbered addresses were not always listed or did not even exist. Phone numbers had only five or six digits and no area codes, just exchanges with names like Yukon and Zenith. There are some other details to note: Garrett & Company is remembered today as the Virginia Dare winery. The Cucamonga Vintage Co. is the Thomas Winery. The numbering system on Foothill Boulevard today is in the thousands, not the hundreds. The A Street in Ontario is now called Holt Boulevard. Guasti did not need street addresses. It was its own little town, with its own post office.

Miss Fruit Industries, dressed as an Old World Italian beauty, represented Guasti sometime in the 1930s. She may have been going to one of the first Wine and Grape Festivals. Pretty girls competing in beauty pageants that named queens and their courts were a common feature at events. Each winery's representative would often dress in costume, usually Italian in nature. (Biane family.)

Crowds of parishioners gather for the Blessing of the Grapes, seen here in 1968. The tradition, dating back hundreds of years, was brought by Secondo Guasti and other Italian immigrants from the old country. The priest at Guasti's church, San Secondo d'Asti, would bless the bounty of the grape harvest. Some of that harvest would be made into sacramental wine, used for communion during Mass at the church.

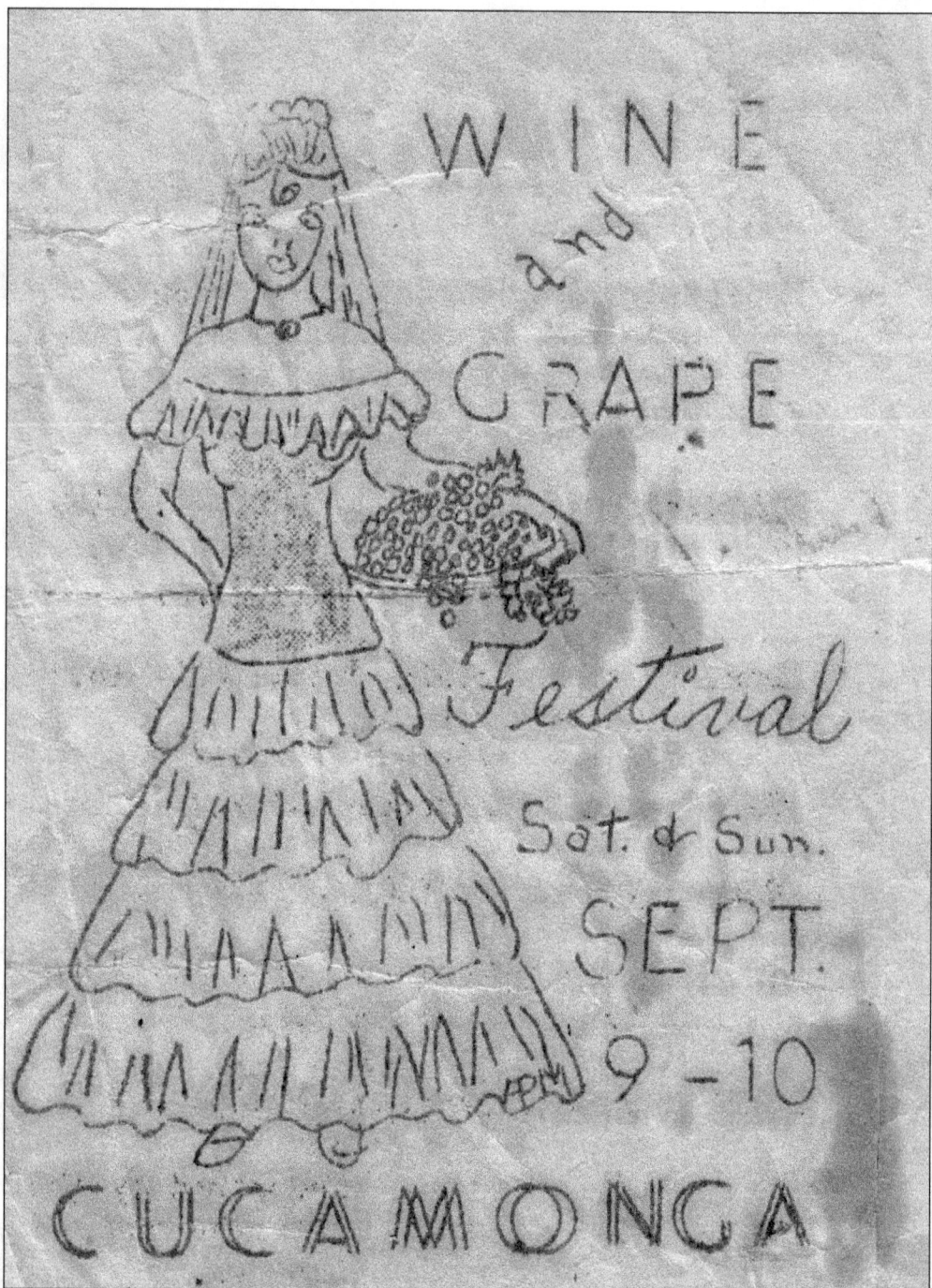

In 1938, the Cucamonga wine district held the first Wine and Grape Festival. The Thomas Winery had been declared the oldest winery in California a few years before, and a grand celebration for its 100th year was planned by service clubs and vintners. This hand-drawn program featuring an Italian signorina set the tradition of the old-country dress for the festival queen and her court. Carnival games, free grapes, and grape juice, as well as good music and dancing, were promised. The tradition of the festival was carried on for over six decades. (Linda Eddy.)

Souvenir Booklet

**Cucamonga District
Wine and Grape Festival**

SEPTEMBER 7-9, 1951

With MAP and HISTORIES of
ALTA LOMA, CUCAMONGA, ETIWANDA
AND GUASTI

By 1951, the festival had become an annual event. Carnivals and professional entertainment, colorful pageants, and amusements for "the little folks" were anticipated each September. In later years, it was called the Grape Harvest Festival. These women are, from left to right, Lynette Hogancamp, Jeannie Campos, Jo Brooks, and Teresa Campos. (Jane Vath O'Connell.)

117

The Grape Queen and her court of 1949 are decked out in full Italian costume in a vineyard. Kneeling in the front is Rosemary Brancacio. The women standing are, from left to right, Lynette Hogancamp, two unidentified, Queen Shirley Honeycutt, Peggy Woodward, and Zita Naverett. (Brancacio-Owen family.)

This photograph of the 1953 Grape Court includes many well-known men of the Cucamonga community. In the first row are, from left to right, Jeanie Camp, Jo Brooks, Charlotte Carrare, Sandra Pastrone, Laura Harrison, Rosemary Brancacio, and Matilda Morra. The men in the second row are, from left to right, Buster Filippi, a Mr. McMahan, unidentified, Carl Masingale, Merral Whitaker, and Scoop Foster. (Brancacio-Owen family.)

Six

FLOOD AND FREEZE

A rare snow-covered Thomas Winery is pictured in 1967. Significant snow in the valley happens once every decade or two. Normally, snow is only seen on the mountaintops a few times a year. Snow in the valley becomes a delightful newsworthy event. The citrus and strawberry farmers probably were not so delighted at the freezing weather, as cold-season crops have begun to sprout. Many of the nation's oranges and lemons are harvested during the temperate California winter. Freezing temperatures can damage or destroy the citrus and other crops. Such temperatures would require farmers to be up all night, lighting smudge pots and running wind machines to keep the fruit from freezing.

Young Shirley Stipe examines the delicate snowfall in Cucamonga early one morning in 1949. The unexpected weather mystifies and delights both young and old Californians, who quickly click photographs as children play in the snow before it melts at midmorning. While her mother was snapping the photograph, Shirley's farmer father was probably checking his fruit trees and other crops for damage from the unusually cold temperatures. (Shirley O'Morrow.)

15055. Cucamonga Mountain, near Los Angeles, California.

Postcards such as this allowed residents to boast of California's mild winters to their families in colder parts of the country. California snow is normally something to look at, not to live in. Many families eagerly moved across the country to escape the Northeast's dark, cold winter months. There is one thing, however, the postcard does not show: the scorching, 100-degree summers.

Cucamonga, "the land of many waters," flooded when heavy rains swelled the creeks to overflowing. In March 1938, the ground was already saturated from heavy storms in February. Another 9.84 inches of rain, two-thirds of the year's average rainfall, poured down in just six days. Roads and bridges were torn apart by torrents of water carrying rocks and boulders down. The powerful floodwaters pushed cars downstream, leaving them swamped in mud. In the West End, seven lives were lost, and $10 million in property loss occurred. At that time, there was no dam at San Antonio Canyon, and the stream cut new channels. The image above shows Baseline Road near Etiwanda. (Both, Lucille Thompson.)

From January 18 to 25, 1969, Southern California was struck by back-to-back subtropical storms that brought death and destruction. The first one brought 4.85 inches of rain. The second storm dumped more than nine inches in three days. Together, it was more than three times the normal rainfall for the month. Earthen dams broke, and floodwaters rushed down the Cucamonga Creek, breaching its banks. Pictured above is the intersection of Vineyard Avenue and Arrow Highway. Homes and businesses from Foothill Boulevard to Sixth Street were inundated. Gov. Ronald Reagan declared Cucamonga a disaster area, and the National Guard was sent in. About 300 people were evacuated, some plucked from rooftops by Marine Corps helicopters.

A fireman fords the rushing water on Hellman Avenue to save stranded flood victims in 1969. Hellman Avenue had long been one of the streets that flooded whenever it rained. In 1914, flooding gutted that roadway seven feet deep. In response, residents built retaining walls and the signature high curbs that still exist in parts of town. (City of Rancho Cucamonga.)

Bridges that crossed the Cucamonga Creek were swept away in 1969, isolating residents and making it difficult to drive around town. The west-facing view in this photograph shows Baseline Road at the Carnelian Avenue bridge crossing. This same bridge washed out in the 1938 flood as well. (Gary Wallace.)

This is the area between Hellman Avenue and Lions Park, on the south side of Baseline Road. North-south streets, such as Beryl Street and Hellman Avenue, routinely flooded during rainstorms. Residents along Hellman Avenue tell of listening to rocks and boulders rumble down the street during rainstorms and of watching unusual items float past—cars, bikes, furniture, even a freezer that was later found downstream with food still inside it. (Gary Wallace.)

Unlike many bridges, the arched Pacific Electric Bridge survived the deluge. The flooded Cucamonga Creek overflowed and rushed down Vineyard Avenue. Money from federal disaster relief helped to finance the construction of a deep flood-control channel down the Cucamonga Wash. Seen here is the Cucamonga Wash prior to the channel being constructed. (Gary Wallace.)

The powerful force of the water pushed cars about like toys. A van on San Bernardino Road (above) and a car on Foothill Boulevard in front of the Thomas Winery (below) became part of the flood debris rammed into whatever was in its path. Rushing water eroded the earth beneath the streets and broke up the asphalt. Not surprisingly, postal service was interrupted in flooded areas. But the mail carriers were instructed to deliver all the mail possible without endangering themselves or their postal vehicles.

The north side of the Thomas Winery (above) and grape-crusher building (below) were hit by the six-foot crest of mud and rock that rushed through the building, causing $250,000 in damages to the newly renovated winery. Due to contact with the floodwaters, 6,000 cases of wines were deemed unsalable. Many of the cases were found downstream. An enormous redwood wine barrel floated off and was found by the railroad tracks a mile away. The Filippi family, the winery's owners, used hair dryers and fans to dry out the 130-year-old adobe walls. The rainy weather persisted. Days later, a second, smaller flood washed through the winery, and the cleaning and drying started over. The Old Homestead building to the east of the winery did not survive the deluge. (Both, City of Rancho Cucamonga.)

Seen in the above photograph, over 10 feet of rocks and debris filled the underpass of the Pacific Electric Railroad tracks at Vineyard and Carnelian Avenues. On the other side of the bridge was the Kapu Kai and Aloha Lanes Bowl. Adults and children had only moments to flee before the surge of water crashed into the building. At least 150 homes were severely damaged or lost. The area from San Bernardino Road to Arrow Highway was without water for several days. A relief station was set up at Sweeten Hall. The Cucamonga Service Club, the Woman's Club, school PTAs, and others collected food, clothes, money, and furniture to help flood victims. The below photograph shows the same underpass today. The high berm on the right separates the Cucamonga Wash from the street. Deep flood-control channels were constructed throughout the city and Southern California to protect residents from another such disaster. (Above, Gary Wallace.)

Visit us at
arcadiapublishing.com